"Observe, ask questions, be curious, dare to throw odd ideas into a group's conversation to make it better. These are all ways to ensure that the blind spots that we all are threatened by do not stay blind. Be an Idea Hunter!"
    —**Ton Büchner**, CEO, Sulzer, Ltd.

"In my company, I ask all of our team members to be business owners. Doing things in a better way, at lower costs, and in a more customer-friendly way requires ideas from everyone. Those ideas come from great Idea Hunters throughout the company, regardless of rank and title. *The Idea Hunter* is not only an enjoyable read; it also offers a practical method so that anyone or any firm can learn the secrets of harnessing the power of ideas to drive success."
    —**Laura J. Sen**, president and CEO, BJ's Wholesale Club

"Humans make progress by discovering new ideas, but also, importantly, by repurposing the ones that already exist. Boynton and Fischer show how each of us can get better at this critical skill—identifying and reapplying existing ideas."
    —**Paul Romer**, senior fellow, Stanford Institute for Economic Policy Research

"Hunting is an apt metaphor. Ideas exist everywhere in the wild. The trick is knowing where to look for them and how to capture them. Boynton and Fischer tell us how."
    —**Ron Sargent**, chairman and CEO, Staples, Inc.

"*The Idea Hunter* is unique. It's about curiosity, agility, and perpetually hunting for better ideas. It's a must-read for anyone who wants to compete and collaborate more effectively each and every day."
    —**Greg Brown**, president and CEO, Motorola Solutions

"This book upends a number of persistent myths about innovation and what it takes to be an 'idea person.' It shows that what's required is not spectacular creativity or remarkable IQ, but curiosity—not innate genius, but a genuine desire to engage in a daily search for ideas. *The Idea Hunter* will help transform the way you and your business operate."
    —**Jay Hooley**, chairman, president, and CEO, State Street Corporation

"Ideas are the lifeblood of innovation, and innovation is the key to growth. Boynton and Fischer offer powerful and practical advice on how to 'jump-shift' the flow of ideas in your organization. This book will become required reading for any leader intent on shaping a high-performance organization."
    —**Michael D. White**, chairman and CEO, DirecTV

The
IDEA
HUNTER

The
IDEA
HUNTER

HOW TO *FIND* THE BEST IDEAS AND MAKE THEM HAPPEN

Andy Boynton and Bill Fischer

with William Bole

JOSSEY-BASS
A Wiley Imprint
www.josseybass.com

Published by Jossey-Bass
A Wiley Imprint
989 Market Street, San Francisco, CA 94103-1741—www.josseybass.com

Library of Congress Cataloging-in-Publication Data

Boynton, Andrew C.
  The idea hunter: how to find the best ideas and make them happen / Andy Boynton and Bill Fischer with William Bole.
     p. cm.
  Includes bibliographical references and index.
ISBN 978-0-470-76776-4 (cloth); ISBN 978-1-118-03884-0 (ebk);
ISBN 978-1-118-03885-7 (ebk); ISBN 978-1-118-03886-4 (ebk)
  1. Creative ability in business. 2. Creative thinking. 3. Success in business. I. Fischer, Bill.
II. Bole, William. III. Title.
  HD53.B69 2011
  650.1—dc22

                                                          2011005783

Printed in the United States of America
FIRST EDITION
HB Printing   10 9 8 7 6 5

CONTENTS

The I–D–E–A Principles

CONTENTS

Asking Marie to marry me was the best idea I ever had!
Kim, Amy, Billy, Sergio, Leah, Nicolas, Isabella,
Mia, and William III are living evidence that one
good idea can give birth to many, many more.

Also, for my mother, Virginia Fumagalli Fischer, who rose
above an eighth-grade education to inspire several generations
with her love for ideas. She was a true Idea Hunter!
—Bill

Dear Jane, you are at the heart of the very best ideas
I've ever had—let's start a fire and watch something tonight
("Maybe a game is on!"), can we go grab some Indian food,
let's take a walk, or let's drive out to Great Point ("and maybe
I can fish for blues!"). You know better than anyone that those
are the ideas I treasure most—and I only enjoy them with you.
—Andy

Why Hunt?

IDEAS MATTER. We could talk at length about the impact of blockbuster ideas, like the microchip and mass production. But one of our favorite examples has to do with something less celebrated: coffee cup lids.

Many people have already forgotten the ritual they used to perform after ordering their latte or double-shot espresso in a coffee shop. Until fairly recently, customers often had to fumble around the counter looking for the right-size lid, because a medium lid would not do if they were holding a large cup of cappuccino. All that changed with the introduction of one-size-fits-all lids, the product of an idea that required some tinkering with the design of the rims of disposable coffee cups.

The notion was just a little one, not often talked about today. But one economist who appreciates such things is Paul Romer of Stanford University. "That small change in the geometry of coffee cups means that somebody can save a little time in setting up the coffee shop, preparing the cups, getting your coffee, and getting out," Romer told an interviewer, explaining how the innovation has touched both the shops and their customers. He points out that millions of little discoveries like this, combined with some very big ones, have exponentially improved the quality of life over the past century.

There's a larger point about the value of ideas big and small. It has to do with the profound difference between a thing and an idea, between a mere object and a creative act. George Bernard Shaw shed light on this distinction. "If you have an apple and I have an apple and we exchange these apples, then you and I will still have one apple," he wrote. "But if you have an idea and I have an idea and we exchange these ideas, then each of us will have two ideas." The apple in your hands will be exactly what it is (until it is bitten into), but your recipe for apple crisp, which is an idea, could be used many times by many people.

Getting back to the coffee shop: the cardboard cup is a thing. Typically a person uses it just once before tossing it into the recycle bin. The lid is also a thing. Yet the insight that one lid could fit cups of all sizes—small, medium, and large—is not a thing. It's an idea. What's more, it's an idea that coffee-shop owners and managers all over the world can reuse over and over again.

Romer takes up an interesting question: Which is a bigger obstacle—a shortage of ideas, or a shortage of things? His research has shown that "idea gaps," as he styles them, hold back progress and innovation much more than the "object gaps." He is speaking primarily about how societies have ultimately risen out of poverty not because of things, like paper or steel, but because of ideas about how to leverage those things (for example, the idea of mass production). His perspective is macroeconomics, but we're looking at this from another angle.

What is more likely to hold us back as individuals—a lack of things, or a lack of ideas? Are many of us falling shy of career goals because our desks aren't big enough or our phones aren't fancy enough? Not likely. Most of us have what we need, as far as that goes. And there are more pressing matters—such as figuring out how to make a more persuasive sales pitch, how to manage a project more effectively, how to ramp up a revenue stream, how to bring a product to market. The most important tools for achieving those ends are in your head and in other heads.

Our focus is on individual managers and professionals: ideas matter to them, now more than ever. You have to know a lot to produce anything of value, whether it's a tangible product or a service. You also have to combine and develop and apply what you know, which requires an idea at every turn. It wouldn't be oversimplifying the matter too much to say that in today's economy, *knowing* things is more important than *making* them. (After all, the back of an iPhone reads: "Designed by Apple in California; Assembled in China." There's a difference.) The idea payoff is greater than the thing payoff for individuals and organizations as well as for societies.

Those who have lingering doubts need look no further than the Google icons on their desktops and the iPods in their pockets. The employees that Google and Apple most value are the ones who understand they're working in an idea-intensive environment. They are valued for what they know and are rewarded for the ideas they've added to such generic items as search engines and MP3 players. They look at things like music players and think of ways to make them more useable and appealing.

But Apple's luminaries and Google's giga-stars are scarcely the only ones who win with ideas. During our travels, we have spent much time talking to customer-facing employees like the housekeepers at Ritz Carlton Hotels. These people are expected (and trained) to look for fresh ideas about how to cater to each guest as an individual customer. They do so, first of all, by noticing things; the word "idea," in fact, is culled from the Greek *idein*, "to see." They look at the twelve crunched-up cans of soda in Andy Boynton's hotel room, pull out pad and pencil, and make a note. This explains why Andy now finds Diet Coke on ice whenever he checks into a room at the Ritz.

Ideas matter to hotel workers. Shouldn't they matter also to people in sales and marketing, and to managers everywhere? The same could be said for teachers, engineers, consultants, and others who get ahead not just by working hard but also by thinking hard. They are idea professionals (whether they describe themselves that way or not). They compete and collaborate more effectively when they know how to find and handle ideas.

And those who do well share one basic strategy. They go Hunting.

INTRODUCTION

Brilliance
Not Required

BREAKAWAY IDEAS COME TO those who are in the habit of looking for them. That is the simple proposition of this book, which maps out a path for professionals of all callings, a way of getting ideas that make a difference. And that way is the Hunt. It's a search for ideas that's open-ended, ongoing, and always personal—dialed into who you are, what projects you're pursuing, and where you're going in your career. What's needed is a fresh batch of skills that professionals can use every day.

Consider the intersecting stories of two passionate Idea Hunters. One is legendary; the other may well become so.

When Walt Disney got the notion of building a great family theme park, he did not go looking for ideas in all the usual places. In his day, the product of choice along that line was the thrill-ride amusement park—a seedy place with bad food and unfriendly employees. This was not Disney's vision of a welcoming environment that would tap into the dreams of children and adults alike, so he went on a search (he was always on the trail of ideas). His quest led him all the way to Tivoli Gardens, a clean and orderly park in Copenhagen with, as one chronicler had put it, "lush flowers, tame rides" and a festive family atmosphere. The television personality

Art Linkletter happened to be with Disney on that trip to Denmark in 1951, which was ostensibly a vacation they took with their wives. "He was making notes all the time—about the lights, the chairs, the seats and the food," Linkletter later recalled. "I asked him what he was doing, and he replied, 'I'm just making notes about something that I've always dreamed of, a great, great playground for the children and families of America.'" The dream became a splendid reality in 1955 with the opening of Disneyland in California.

Walt Disney once quipped that he was in the business of "selling happiness." Entrepreneur Puneet Nanda is in the same business but in an entirely different industry. He is better known as Dr. Fresh, president and CEO of a California-based dental hygiene company by the same name that makes products with special appeal to children. His most popular item is the FireFly, a toothbrush with flashing lights that blink for sixty seconds. The Indian immigrant did not find the idea on a list of the "Top 100 Ideas for Dental Products and Accessories." He got it from his daughter, who was four years old at the time and no more enthusiastic about brushing her teeth than any other four-year-old. One day he told his daughter that they had to go do some chores. Her response was that she'd go only if she could find her sneakers with the flashing lights. That's when the light went off in his head. He drove out to Disneyland, bought a few pairs of blinking magnet earrings, and taped them to his daughter's toothbrush. When they arrived back home, she brushed intently for eight minutes straight.

The brightly colored FireFly, sold in retail stores nationwide, is now the linchpin of a $44.3-million company. Nanda has become the consummate Hunter, devoting half his time to drumming up new ideas for product innovations.

Just looking at these snapshots, you could tease out a few lessons about Idea Hunters:

- They know their gig—what they're all about as professionals and where they're heading. Selling happiness in a healthy and wholesome way is what lends identity to both the legendary Disney brand and the up-and-coming Dr. Fresh.
- They don't let the organization, job, industry, or profession define their Idea Hunt. Certainly Disney did not follow in those tracks when his trusted advisers, including his brother and partner Roy, ridiculed the notion of a "Mickey Mouse Park," partly because it ran afoul of the thrill-ride-amusement-park paradigm. Nanda clearly was not just listening to colleagues at dental trade shows when he designed a whole line of products (including flossing containers) with blinking lights. Each went down his own idea trail.
- They recognize how the world around them connects with their plans and projects. Disney was ready to learn, with notebook in hand, when he strolled through the gates of Tivoli Gardens while vacationing in Denmark. Nanda turned his daughter's fascination with flashing sneakers—nothing out of the ordinary—into a breakthrough when he connected it to his vision and projects. In fact, he hasn't stopped looking to children for ideas. He holds a national contest each year, challenging kids in the second through fifth grades to invent their fantasy toothbrush. The winner in 2008 was a South Carolina girl who designed a toothbrush that speaks, reminding people to turn off the tap while they brush their teeth. She won a free trip to Disneyland.

Already Out There

Disneyland and the FireFly were products of idea work—which, contrary to popular impression, isn't something done only by uniquely gifted "creative types." Idea work is a vital asset for all professionals today. It is highly learnable—and that doesn't mean learning to become a creative genius, because, as we'll see in these pages, high-value ideas are not necessarily created. More often than not, they're already out there, waiting to be spotted and then shaped into an innovation.

The idea that launched the iPod was way out there and reeled in by Phil Schiller. A marketing executive (not a techie), Schiller did not dream up the notion of a click wheel—the lightning-fast scroll wheel that helped separate the iPod from its poor MP3 cousins. He borrowed this feature from a motley assortment of electronics products dating to the early 1980s, and by slapping the idea onto Apple's music player, Schiller secured his place in the annals of innovation (more on this in Chapter Three). As this feat illustrates, ideas aren't generated so much as they're found and then something useful is done with them. That's why we proudly appropriate the words of Thomas Edison—who described his search for solutions as "the Hunt."

Brilliance is optional. What we have found in our work and research is that the most successful Idea Hunters are not, as a rule, geniuses. Rather, they are just idea-active. They have a voracious appetite for acquiring ideas, and they are skilled at setting those ideas in motion—selling them and making them happen. They think like Miles Davis, the legendary jazz trumpeter and band leader, who once remarked, "I'm happy if I could play one new idea on a night."

How do you become an Idea Hunter, someone who stands out with ideas in an increasingly crowded professional marketplace? It begins with embracing a new perspective on the innovative work most prized by organizations and clients today. We have seen many people arrive at such a fresh outlook in the course of our DeepDive sessions, a process of idea-storming and solution-shaping that we developed for corporate teams worldwide (and that is now trademarked by Deloitte Consulting). No matter how smart they think they are, individual participants in these sessions come to realize that there are more ideas at the table than there are in their own brains. Teams come to find that there are more ideas in the room than there are at their tables, and still more in the building, in the city, and beyond. They discover the practical value of a deliberate, persistent, wide-ranging search for ideas.

Based in part on these experiences, we have identified four bedrock principles for use by managers and other professionals. We call these the I-D-E-A principles, each of which connects with crucial attitudes, habits, skills, and strategies.

The first principle turns on the question: Do I want to be *interested*, or merely *interesting*? All of us naturally want to be interesting, but in the Hunt for ideas, being *Interested* in the world around you is of equal or greater importance. Those who excel at the Hunt understand that almost anyone can hand them an incredible idea, which they are generally free to use. Because they are thinkers as well as doers, the best Idea Hunters also understand that intellectual curiosity is not irrelevant to business success. Idea people approach their work with drive and enthusiasm, but also with a level of intellectual seriousness. They agree with Warren Buffett, who believes (as his business partner Charlie Munger relates) that it's "very hard to succeed in something unless you take the first step—which is to become very interested in it." And, we would quickly add, to become very interested in other people, too. As we show in the examples of innovators like Sam Walton, curiosity will take you further toward your goals than cleverness or even brilliance.

The second principle is about diversification. Idea Hunters are aware of the multitude of trails that can lead to worthwhile ideas. When setting out on a search, they always take along an assorted mix of idea sources, a collection as *Diverse* as any investment portfolio. This is how to avoid the plague of "me too" ideas that come from traveling the same narrow paths as everyone else in your group or field. You don't want to be where all of the competition is—browsing the same publications, going to the same web sites, comparing notes with the same people, and winding up with variations (at best) of the same tired ideas. You want to bring in thoughts that are different but applicable, seemingly unrelated but potentially valuable—whether the source is a member of your team at work or the guy who coaches your daughter's softball team. This part of idea work requires a wide intellectual bandwidth and a desire to span distances—for example, between your specialty and other specialties. That's how you go about launching what management superguru Tom Peters calls "WOW projects." The operative assumption should be that ideas are everywhere.

The third principle says you need to exercise your idea muscles all the time, not just when you're in a brainstorming session at work. The most experienced Idea Hunters are *Exercised*, engaged in daily training, though it's hardly a chore for them because they take pleasure in the Hunt. Many of them keep notebooks where they record what they've seen and heard, and they connect their personal experiences and impressions to their projects and proposals. Their search is highly focused and purpose-driven. They'll scan web sites that they have determined are most likely to provoke interesting, adaptable ideas, yet they remain open to serendipity—to the idea that seems to come out of nowhere. One key to being exercised is to develop the skills of observation, which include knowing what needs to be observed closely. These skills go hand in hand with other habits of the Hunt, such as recording your observations (with or without a notebook) and sketching out rough notions that you can bounce off friends and colleagues. Successful Idea Hunters develop these and many other habits, realizing that the pursuit of ideas doesn't start when you're faced with a difficult problem that needs a quick solution. If you wait until then, it'll be too late.

The fourth principle is that you also need to be *Agile* in your handling of ideas. You can't expect to proceed in a straight line, snatching up a single idea and taking it to market. That could happen (theoretically), but more likely, you'll need to veer left and right, catching and combining ideas that come at you from different directions, always with an eye on your projects and your gig. Ideas require deft handling, partly because of the sheer number of them that need to be in play. (As Edison said, "To get a good idea, you must first get a lot of ideas.") Agility is required especially because these notions and impressions are worth little unless they're in motion, shifting in response to fresh data and conversation, evolving through stages of reflection and prototyping. That's why, through much of the Hunt, wild ideas are encouraged, bad ideas are not a deal breaker, and quantity is preferred over quality. The successful Hunter knows that the most important thing is to keep up the idea flow.

If you're looking for a brisk way of calling up these four principles, just think *Interested, Diverse, Exercised,* and *Agile,* or simply I-D-E-A.

Ready to Unlearn

This book is about learning, but it's also about unlearning. It's about altering some of our mental pictures—including the one in which we discover an idea by shutting the office door and thinking real hard, finger pressed tightly against forehead. Hard thinking is, of course, necessary, and sometimes you need to close the door. But there are better ways of visualizing the Hunt, which looks more like a search party in which more than one set of eyes is needed. Or picture the common areas at work, where good conversation happens (especially if you make it happen); or the conference room in

Cupertino, California, where Schiller and the Apple team decided that a scroll wheel was the right user interface for their music player. Idea finding isn't really about sitting back and searching your brain. It's much closer to a contact sport.

Still, there are commanding images in our culture that can throw you off track. The most abiding image is that of a light bulb going off above the head, the "Aha!" moment when somebody, safely distanced from the nearest human being (or any external stimuli), comes up with a scathingly brilliant notion. Of course, the incandescent light bulb was pioneered by none other than Edison, the very symbol of the tinkering genius alone (supposedly) in his lab. Yet, as will be further told in these pages, every one of his matchless innovations was a product of elbow-to-elbow collaboration. Part of the intent of this book is to help turn off the light-bulb theory of how an idea is found. We need new attitudes and strategies for the idea work each of us is poised to do.

At the core of this book, we unpack the basic traits of highly successful Idea Hunters, whose attitudes and actions embody the four I-D-E-A Principles (Chapters Two through Five). To help illustrate these traits, we turn to an eclectic band of Idea Hunters—ranging from Thomas Edison to Warren Buffett to the Arctic explorers, and others famous and not so famous—who will be our colorful guides.

Along these trails, we thrash out other features of the Hunt. Knowing your gig is a prerequisite. Without a sense of purpose and goals, you won't know what you're looking for and you'll be defenseless against the demons of information overload. In Chapter One, we explain how to discern your gig and make it work for you, and we return to this theme at several other turns. Creating great conversations is another staple of idea work. The strategic value of conversations is apparent throughout the book, and in Chapter Six we take a close look at how to launch and continue the most effective conversations.

We also present "IdeaWork" recommendations following each of the I-D-E-A chapters. These items deal successively with how to (1) "sell the best hour of the day to yourself" for continued learning, (2) take on the vital characteristics of a generalist even if you (like most of us) are specialists in one sense or another, (3) develop and maintain a portfolio of idea sources, and (4) launch a fully developed idea. Finally, in the Epilogue, we offer tools for helping you take stock of your progress in the course of The Idea Hunt. This is, to no small degree, a measure of attitude, of the realization that the best ideas exist outside of your brain and are there for the taking.

So let the learning—and the unlearning—begin.

CHAPTER 1

Know Your Gig

THE IDEA HUNT BEGINS with a desire to learn about the world around you, but a good stride in that direction is to know a few things about yourself. Later on we will showcase the value of being interested, of being constantly on the lookout for ideas, of being a learning machine. But what is the energy that fires up your interest and curiosity, the power source for such a machine? What is the fuel that drives the Hunt?

Our answer is the *gig*. By this, we are not referring to what a musician does on a Saturday night or to a job picked up by a freelance graphic designer. Our notion of the gig is much broader. It's closer to one's personal brand or professional identity, even to the sense of vocation that many people seek to nurture. We're talking about your gig in life or, more specifically, in your professional life. We're talking about the Big Gig.

The Introduction offered a glimpse of one famously successful gig: Walt Disney's. His gig was to create entertainment for the whole family, whether through amusement parks like Disneyland or animated films like *Fantasia*. There are similar passions and purposes to be gleaned from every celebrated Idea Hunter's story. Henry Ford's gig was to create a car for everyone, and he had to refashion the process of manufacturing to do it. Warren Buffett's distinction, apart from his piggy bank, is that he took a different tack on investing than his colleagues. He sought to understand the fundamentals of a company rather than try to predict the ups and downs of the stock market.

Those icons knew their gigs. And the salient point is that their gigs gave focus and direction to their learning and idea seeking. Because he was interested in family-friendly entertainment, Disney did not go looking for his best ideas in the seamy American amusement parks of his time. He traveled to Denmark instead, to observe the scene at Tivoli Gardens, an amusement park full of fresh flowers and happy-faced revelers of all ages. Buffett didn't pass his days staring at the ticker tape or conjuring up ways to game the market. He set his mind to learning whatever he could about a specific firm or industry. That served his goal of finding stocks that sold below the real worth of the company.

A gig is not defined by someone's line of work, much less by a job title. It's not even a formal specialization, although it does reflect a distinctive way of adding value to one's work. A product developer's gig is not product development; rather, it might be to encourage the free flow of ideas in a unit or organization, to help build a culture of conversation. A sales associate's gig is not sales; it might instead rest on a capacity for empathy, a talent for getting beneath the surface and understanding a customer's needs.

A schoolteacher's gig might be to serve as a teachers' leader—by heading up a committee, leading a school team, forming a discussion group, or chairing a department. She might take on these and other roles with an eye to becoming an administrator or a professional-development expert. As this latter example illustrates, gigs also have a future dimension—where you're heading. National Public Radio's Scott Simon has spoken of his father's advice: "Dress for the gig you want, not the one you have." The elder

Simon was a comedian, but his advice applies to almost everyone. When you're looking for ideas and new things to learn, think about your vision. Think about who you'd like to become, as a professional—and align your learning with that picture of yourself. The teacher, for example, might want to develop conversations with others who have made the transition from working with peers to leading them.

Knowing your gig is a major step forward on the idea trail. It's the big steering wheel of your interest and curiosity. Even if you already have a clear conception of your gig, it's important to occasionally refresh it, because circumstances change and new opportunities arise. But how does one discern or reassess a gig? In short, doing so requires self-reflection—grappling with questions about your passions and talents. And then it's necessary to connect your answers to the professional marketplace. Put simply: is there a customer for what you're offering?

Here we would like to borrow questions from two people prominent in different fields, drawing on different sources of wisdom. The first is an iconoclastic management guru; the second is a theologian.

The Discernment

In *The Brand You 50*, author and speaker Tom Peters recalls browsing an advice book about work and bumping into a sentence that jolted him: "When was the last time you asked, 'What do I want to be?'" Thinking it through, Peters devised four questions that could be asked in arriving at a self-definition. The first is the what-I-want-to-be question that made an instant impression on him. The others are: What do I want to stand for? Does my work matter? And, am I making a difference?

13

Other clusters of questions are posed by Peters in other contexts relating to one's products and projects. For example: "Who are you? What is your product? How is it special? How is it different from others' similar offerings? How can I demonstrate its trustworthiness? How can I demonstrate I'm 'with it'/contemporary?" Thoughtful answers to even just a few such questions will help bring your gig more clearly into focus.

Michael Himes, a Catholic priest and professor of theology at Boston College, has given considerable thought to how a student or anyone else discerns a vocation or calling in life. In a number of articles and presentations, he has outlined three basic questions people can reflect on, when they're making choices about a profession or even just a job or some other role. Those questions are:

1. Is this a source of joy?
2. Is this something that taps into your talents and gifts—engages all of your abilities—and uses them in the fullest way possible?
3. Is this role a genuine service to the people around you, to society at large?

Himes has an even pithier version of this self-examination:

1. Do you get a kick out of it?
2. Are you any good at it?
3. Does anyone want you to do it?

"Do I get a kick out of it?" has to be answered by you, the person asking the question. Himes says one way of answering is to think about the issues and concerns that you return to over and over. These are what "fascinate you . . . excite you . . . really intrigue you . . . lure you on. They get you to ask more and more questions."

On the other hand, "Are you any good at it?" is a question for people around you to answer. In this connection, Himes recommends fostering a circle of friends who can be honest with you about your talents. Perhaps a simpler way of going about this would be to consider the people who have been important to you and your career—let's say teachers, bosses, colleagues, clients. What have you learned from them about yourself, about your skills and the areas in which you excel? What do you suppose they would say if someone were to ask them about your strengths and weaknesses? We would add that the discernment also has to be about potential. It's not simply a matter of what you're good at now, but what you might become good at—no, great at—in the future.

According to Himes, "Does anyone want you to do it?" must be answered by the people you are serving (or would like to serve). "We must hear from the people around us what they really need. What is it that they want us to do?" This is vocation talk. In workaday terms, it's all about the "customer," elastically defined to include employers, clients, team members, and others. Will they go for the package of skills, perspectives, and approaches that I'd like to sell? Am I offering something that will help make their lives a little easier, their products more valuable, their projects more successful? And will they recognize this?

Discerning your vocation is not exactly the same as understanding your gig. You may have chosen long ago to become a product developer (your vocation), before realizing that you'd like to be, or already are, the one who spearheads conversations about ideas for new products (your gig). Still, the three vocational questions are handy tools for discerning a gig. We would tweak them as follows:

1. What is it that constantly grabs my interest and sparks my curiosity?
2. What am I good at? And what do I want to be great at?
3. And where's the market for this?

Take a moment to reflect on these questions, and keep in mind that they're not really about reinventing yourself. They're about reflecting on what you're already doing, thinking, planning, desiring.

Part of the discernment is to think about the distinctive value you add to your work, the special skills and perspectives you bring to the task. If you're an accountant, what separates you from the one who works two floors above you? What makes you stand out? Or, how would you *like to* stand out? What's your vision of how to become the best accountant around? Peters has offered a straightforward assessment tool for examining these questions. Fill in the blanks: "I am known for [2–4 things]. By this time next year, I plan to be known for [1–2 more things]." This will get you pretty close to sizing up your added value as a professional, now and in the near future.

Another path of discernment is to craft a personal mission statement that gets to the core of what you value. Peters recommends something in writing that takes stock of your priorities: How exactly do you spend your time? What's the nature of your contributions at a meeting? Who exactly do you hang out with? A personal statement of this sort could provoke and clarify ideas about what Peters calls The Brand You—that is, what distinguishes you as a professional. It's important, though, to keep in mind that a gig should never be written in stone. Like a vocation, a gig is not static. It requires continued self-reflection and revision, because passions change, knowledge expands, and needs shift. As Himes often says in his talks to college students, "The only time your vocation is settled is when you are settled (six feet under that is!)." Ditto for the gig.

The Circle of Competence

Warren Buffett is well known for steering clear of high-tech stocks. He says he has no business in that arena—because he doesn't understand it. His wariness on that score is part of a principle that he has articulated together with his investment partner Charlie Munger. And that is the importance of keeping within your "circle of competence" (an application of Himes's second question, "Am I any good at it?"). Buffett knows not just his gig, but his circle of competence. That takes him a long way toward figuring out what he should be doing and where he should be searching for ideas.

It's easy to think that a phenomenally successful investor like Buffett must be taking some big risks. You could picture him swinging at almost every pitch, trying to hit balls hurled over his head or into the dirt. This is not, however, his stance as an investor. He works differently, and the baseball analogy is not an idle one. An ardent fan, Buffett often speaks of Ted Williams, the famed Red Sox slugger who revealed the secret of his success in his book *The Science of Hitting*. Nicknamed the "Splendid Splinter," his approach was to carve the strike zone into seventy-seven cells, each one the size of a baseball. He swung at the balls that landed in his best cells, and let the others whizz by, even if it meant being called out on strikes once in a while. As Buffett once remarked at a shareholders' meeting, Williams knew that "waiting for the fat pitch would mean a trip to the Hall of Fame. Swinging indiscriminately would mean a ticket to the minors."

Buffett and his firm Berkshire Hathaway have exerted the same discipline in their investment strategies. They don't lunge at opportunities outside their areas of proficiency. "If we have a strength," Buffett has explained, "it is in recognizing when we are operating well within our circle of competence and when we are approaching the perimeter." Munger adds: "Warren and I don't feel like we have any great advantage in the high-tech sector. In fact, we feel like we're at a big disadvantage in trying to understand the nature of technical developments in software, computer chips, or what have you. So we tend to avoid that stuff, based on our personal inadequacies." Among other virtues, this demonstrates the value of humility— acknowledging what you don't know. It's also a powerful idea. "Everybody has a circle of competence. And it's going to be very hard to enlarge that circle," Munger advises in his Benjamin Franklin– style book *Poor Charlie's Almanack*. In this way Buffett and Munger are simply echoing Thomas Watson Sr., the storied founder of IBM: "I'm no genius. I'm smart in spots, and I stay around those spots."

Another outfit that understands its circle of competence is Google. A touchstone of the company's philosophy is that it's best to do one thing really, really well, as described in the company's "Our Philosophy" web page:

> We do search. With one of the world's largest research groups focused exclusively on solving search problems, we know what we do well, and how we could do it better. Through continued iteration on difficult problems, we've been able to solve complex issues and provide continuous improvements to a service that already makes finding information a fast and seamless experience for millions of people. Our dedication to improving search helps us apply what we've learned to new products, like Gmail and Google Maps. Our hope is to bring the power of search to previously unexplored areas, and to help people access and use even more of the ever-expanding information in their lives.

On the surface, this may sound like a straightforward statement of specialization, and to a degree it is. But the emphasis on "continuous improvements" and reaching into "unexplored areas" is not a call to simple, narrow specialization. The circle of competence is more than that. It's not just a way of saying, if you're a physician: "I'm a heart specialist." It's a way of considering your strengths and weaknesses as a heart specialist, and where you might be able to stand out, in that field. And, as the Google statement indicates, it's also about learning and applying the insights to new areas or subareas.

On this point, we are somewhat less skeptical than Munger and Buffett, who underscore the difficulty of enlarging the circle of competence. We believe the emphasis should be on *widening* the circle through constant learning and deep interest in matters related to your gig (or your next gig). Buffett himself has expanded his range of mastery by learning everything he needed to know about spheres of investment that were new to him, like the newspaper industry. Of course, he made sure to do the learning first, before the investing.

Gigs Matter

What Buffett and all effective Idea Hunters understand is that the gig is a general filter. It screens out some of the information and ideas that cascade your way, making it easier to repel the demons of information overload. It helps guide you to what you need to be learning and to the ideas you need to be getting. Buffett doesn't have to scatter his valuable learning time across the market, because he knows that certain sectors, such as high-tech, are not what he's good at. He could happily leave that to others.

The gig usually stays in the back of your mind, but it's always there. When fully assimilated, it's an ever-present preoccupation, a switch that goes on automatically, often unconsciously, no matter what you're doing. You could be reading, or at the movies, or talking to somebody. All of a sudden, time slows down, and you're in a zone where you're connecting what you're hearing to the few things you're always switched-on about. Other times you might make the connections later on.

A person can have more than one gig. A professor could be known for a particular method of teaching as well as her distinct contributions to an academic research field, just as an Internet technology specialist can also be an aspiring entrepreneur. The schoolteacher who's a teacher of teachers is also, needless to say, a teacher of students; she should have a gig for that too.

There are also entire categories of gigs. For example, there are some people—inventors, like Edison—who focus entirely on creating new things. In pursuit of his gig, Edison prided himself on exhaustive experimentation, and even failure, along the road to discovery. (His gig was not mere invention, though he was plenty good at that; it was creating things that people really need and that are marketable.)

There are others, like Buffett, whose gigs fall into the category of improving things—in his case, the way people make decisions about investing. Still other gigs are marked by their breadth. On the one hand, Walt Disney was squarely focused on family-friendly entertainment. But this gig pointed him and his successors in a rich variety of directions, ranging from amusement parks to film animation to vacation cruises.

Finally, there is a foundational gig for practically everyone. Here again, we could apply one of Michael Himes's themes. He points out that people have multiple vocations (he is, for instance, a priest, a theologian, a teacher, a writer, a friend, an uncle, and so on). But he says one vocation embraces all the others—to be a human being. "All of my other vocations, all of the many ways in which I live my life, must contribute to that one all-embracing demand, that one constant vocation to be fully, totally, absolutely as human as I can possibly be," he writes. We feel that in today's economy, there is a universal gig that encompasses all the other gigs, and that is to be an idea professional. This meta-gig is nothing less than a question of identity and self-definition.

The accountant is not really, at bottom, an accountant. She is an idea professional, or more precisely, someone who Hunts for ideas. And part of belonging to this burgeoning class of individuals is to understand that there are not one but two products of the work that people do. The first is the actual thing we make or the service we provide or the process we manage. The second product, no less essential, is what we learn along the way. It's the ideas we get about how to do a better job and strengthen our gig. This calls for a new attitude. And it is, in our view, part of everyone's professional calling. Everyone is an Idea Hunter.

Interested

D
E
A

CHAPTER 2

Be Interested, Not Just Interesting

HENRY FORD IS REMEMBERED as the industrialist who in-troduced the Model T—the jet-black car that forever changed the way Americans wheel around, simply because it was affordable (thanks to another Ford innovation, the assembly line). Less mem-orably, Ford was also an aficionado of auto racing: he both designed and drove fast cars. One day in 1905, he was attending a motor race in Palm Beach where a smash-up left a French car in pieces. Inter-ested in more than just the spectacle, Ford walked over to the crash site after the race.

He investigated the pile of steel and rubber. "I picked up a little valve strip stem. It was very light and very strong. I asked what it was made of. Nobody knew," Ford recounted in his auto-biography *My Life and Work*. "I gave the stem to my assistant. 'Find out all about this,' I told him. 'That is the kind of material we ought to have in our cars.'" It turned out to be a steel alloy that contained vanadium, which was not manufactured in the United States at the time.

Ford may have embellished this account for dramatic effect, but as biographer Steven Watts points out, there's no doubt about the significance of Ford's finding. Vanadium steel provided the "final, crucial piece of the production puzzle" of how to construct a durable, lightweight car at a low price, Watts explains in his book *The People's Tycoon*: *Henry Ford and the American Century*. That Model T was introduced three years later, after much brainstorming, development, and prototyping.

There's much about this tale that illustrates the ways of an Idea Hunter. It portrays someone who knew his gig—his mission, his passion—which in Ford's case was to mold a new production process to manufacture a car for everyone. It reveals a person who was quick to recognize how seemingly unrelated occurrences—a crash scene in Palm Beach or the English laboratory that experimented with vanadium—could connect with his plans and projects. But more than anything else, this story highlights the importance of being interested in the world out there. This is the first principle of The Idea Hunt.

Note that being *interested* is not the same as being *interesting*. Ford did not, as far as we know, wander over to the crash scene in order to impress others with his knowledge of automobile production or to regale them with stories of his feats as a race-car driver. He simply followed his curiosity to the scene.

Spotting the people who are genuinely interested is easy. Often you can see it in their body language and hear it in the questions they're asking. Kurt Barnard, a retailing consultant in New York, told of his first encounter with Sam Walton, in 1967. "When he meets you, he looks at you—head cocked to one side, forehead slightly creased—and he proceeds to extract every piece of information in your possession. He always makes little notes. And he pushes on and on," Barnard recalled. "After two and a half hours, he left, and I was totally drained. I wasn't sure what I had just met, but I was sure we would hear more from him."

The world did hear more from Sam Walton, who built the Wal-Mart empire at least partly on the intensity of his interest in other people's ideas. He traveled from Arkansas to Manhattan and points in between just to hear what people were saying about pricing, distribution, inventory, and other markers of his trade. As Walton once explained, this was one way he and the early Wal-Mart managers tried to "make up for our lack of experience and sophistication." Whether they're in retail or any other line, people get ideas by cultivating a capacity for interest and the habit of intellectual curiosity.

In a professional context, intellectual curiosity is basically an abiding interest in any and all matters that could improve the job you're doing. Conventional wisdom holds that the cleverer you are, the better your ideas. But in our experience the cleverest people—important as they are in an organization—have a tendency to overestimate their brain power. Without the added component of curiosity, they stick to their success formula and may not go hunting for better ideas. In other words, they're just not interested enough.

Curiosity, on the other hand, can more than make up for a lack of brilliance. No less a trailblazer than Albert Einstein once made the disarming comment, "I have no special talents. I am only passionately curious." This is often the most striking characteristic of a highly successful person. Consider this firsthand description of Scott Cook, founder and CEO of Intuit, by the writer Michael S. Hopkins: "Listening, he seems to forget himself. He seems composed of pure curiosity. He's like a man who always expects that the next thing someone—anyone—tells him might be the most surprising and enlightening thing he's heard. He listens without blinking. He learns."

A curious mind is on the lookout for surprises. It embraces them and finds a way to learn from them. Such thinking has a leavening effect on how we look at things, because when we are curious, we are less likely to take something for granted. We look at an ordinary happening and see something extraordinary. This opens a path to innovation, partly because an ordinary idea in one setting could prove remarkable if applied to another setting.

Curiosity at the Trading Post

In the early twentieth century, hundreds of thousands of people journeyed far to take part in the Canadian fur trade. Many saw how inhabitants of the northerly regions stored their food in the winter—by burying the meats and vegetables in the snow. But probably few of them entertained thoughts about how this custom might relate to other fields of endeavor. One who did was a young man named Clarence Birdseye, who spent four years on a fur-trading expedition that began in 1912. He was amazed to find that freshly caught fish and duck, frozen quickly in such a fashion, retained their taste and texture. He started wondering: Why can't we sell food in the United States that operates on the same basic principle? With such thoughts, an industry was born.

Birdseye developed the means of freezing foods rapidly, and then sold his ideas and processes to General Foods in 1930. (He later developed inexpensive freezer displays that enabled a system of distribution.) His name—adapted for brand purposes as Birds Eye—is still seen by all who open freezer doors in supermarkets.

The father of frozen foods made something extraordinary from what, for the northern folk, was the ordinary practice of preserving food in the frozen ground. We do not know exactly what went on in Birdseye's mind when he observed this means of storage, but the thinking process is described well by Tom Peters. "Something mysterious happens to a curious, fully engaged mind," he writes in *The Brand You 50*. "Strange little sparks are set off, connections made, insights triggered. The results: an exponentially increased ability to tune up/reinvent/Wow-ize today's project at work." In other words, curiosity is a way of adding value to what you see. Birdseye's curiosity was strong enough to lift him out of the routine way of seeing things. It set the stage for innovation and discovery, for coming up with something new.

There's an additional—and critical—facet to the frozen-foods discovery: The idea came from already existing practice. It wasn't manufactured out of thin air or spontaneously generated in the brain of a creative genius. Birdseye took the same cognitive route that countless Idea Hunters have taken: He noticed an idea in one environment and transplanted it into a different one. His curiosity added phenomenal value to what he saw, but the idea was already out there.

Sometimes ideas just need to be found and replicated. One-size-fits-all coffee lids, for example, must be universal by now. They're a simple case of reuse. People all over the world have used and reused this idea, without altering it substantially, just as people might use a particular casserole recipe. This act, by itself, has an enormously productive impact on people's work and entire economies.

Birdseye, however, saw an idea and found a dramatically different purpose for it. This is the full repurposing of an idea. And this is what Phil Schiller did when he and the team at Apple were looking for the right user interface for their music player, which was on the drawing boards at the time. Presumably his mind flashed back to the early 1980s when Hewlett Packard put out its Workstation computer, which sported a scroll wheel. And this went on to become a pronounced feature of the first iPod. That's repurposing. The exact cost of such a discovery? Zero. That's the leveraging power of ideas.

Learning Machines

Interest and curiosity lead to learning. And learning gives rise to ideas—thoughts of any kind that can spark an innovation or simply a better product or process. There has to be a passion for learning. Without it, there is no flow of ideas.

When we speak of learning, we are not thinking primarily of formal education—what's taught in a classroom or at an executive training session. The most useful picture of learning is not a school desk or a PowerPoint presentation. More evocative is the image of a hunter or seeker. Some of the most forward-looking managers today are those who attach a value to learning that borders on intellectual or even religious devotion. One such seeker is Tim O'Reilly, a Silicon Valley entrepreneur and founder and CEO of O'Reilly Media, who has stayed ahead of the technological curve for decades. He created, for example, the first commercial web site back in 1992, and he invested in e-books long before others even thought of making money in that domain.

O'Reilly devotes most of his time to the search for ideas—scanning the Internet, checking blogs, discussing trends with other entrepreneurs. He says one goal of his company is to demonstrate that being a business person can "represent a means of exploring the world, one that is just as profound as religious inquiry or Greek philosophy or New Age introspection," as reporter Max Chafkin related in *Inc.* magazine. For entrepreneurs like O'Reilly, exploration is not optional; it's the raw material of innovation.

This kind of learning is not episodic. It is constant. It's what Warren Buffett does. He is acclaimed as the richest super-investor in the world, but is perhaps less known as someone dedicated to the proposition that ideas matter. There's a simple reason why he seeks out knowledge every day: he knows of no other strategy for remarkable success. "If Warren had stopped learning early on, his record would be a shadow of what it's been," explains his friend Charlie Munger.

Apart from his association with the "Oracle of Omaha," Munger is one of the preeminent investors of our time, and one of the wisest. Speaking at the University of Southern California's law school commencement in May 2007, he told the graduates, "Without lifetime learning, you people are not going to do very well. You are not going to get very far in life based on what you already know." He noted that Buffett's investment skills had increased markedly in the twelve years since he turned sixty-five, because of continued learning.

"I constantly see people rise in life who are not the smartest, sometimes not even the most diligent," Munger said at USC. "But they are learning machines. They go to bed every night a little wiser than they were when they got up. And boy, does that help, particularly when you have a long run ahead of you." With Munger and Buffett, as for everyone else, it all starts with being interested. "I could force myself to be fairly good in a lot of things but I couldn't be really good at anything where I didn't have an intense interest."

The intensity of Buffett's interest is revealed in his whole way of investing. He came up at a time when most investors practiced a version of voodoo economics, playing the market much as they would a Ouija board or a slot machine. (Some might say that for many investors today, old habits have been difficult to break, in this respect.) Learning from his mentor, Benjamin Graham of Columbia University, Buffett fixed his attention not just on the waxing and waning of a company's stock, but primarily on its deeper value, as indicated by such measures as earnings and assets.

Searching for the "intrinsic value" of a company, Buffett would conduct research of a kind few others did on their own, often heading down in person to Moody's or Standard & Poor's during his early days in New York. Buffett later recalled, "I was the only one who ever showed up at those places. They never asked if I was a customer. I would get these files that dated back forty or fifty years. They didn't have copy machines, so I'd sit there and scribble all these little notes, this figure and that figure."

He also looked for ideas and market clues in conventional ways, like reading annual reports and the *Wall Street Journal*, but often with a splash of difference. In the 1980s, in Omaha, he went so far as to strike a special deal with the local distributor of the *Journal*, as Alice Schroeder relates in her riveting biography *The Snowball: Warren Buffett and the Business of Life*. "When batches of the *Journal* arrived in Omaha every night, a copy was pulled out and placed in his driveway before midnight. He sat up waiting to read tomorrow's news before everybody else got to see it," she writes.

This extreme devotion aside, the value he placed on reading his favorite newspaper is illustrative partly because it is so ordinary and easy to emulate. Journalist Mattathias Schwartz said it well in *Harper's* magazine: "The story of Warren Buffett has long been a siren song to millions of other desk sitters who believe that, through regular reading of the *Wall Street Journal*, an average intelligence can beat the Dow."

All the while, Buffett has been a consummate borrower of ideas. It was a practice he referred to as "riding coattails," linking up with mentors like Graham and others who had useable ideas, even small ones aimed at netting relatively modest amounts of money.

There's much more that can be said about Warren Buffett as an Idea Hunter, and more will be said in these pages. But from these observations we can start drawing a picture of how one extraordinary learning machine operates:

- Buffett has devoted at least as much time to thinking and learning as he does to doing. With just a little exaggeration, Munger notes that Buffett spends about half his time sitting and reading and the other half talking to people he trusts.
- He has a thoroughgoing approach to getting ideas. He talks to smart people and conducts his research—quantitative, quali-

tative, and the rummaging-through-dusty-shelves variety—in areas where no one else thinks to look. He has organized his life around gathering information leading to ideas he could use.

- His idea search is highly purposeful. He didn't just browse the *Journal*. He wangled a copy of each edition before anyone else did, which means he was able to get ideas earlier than other investors. More to the point, he focused his search on ideas that would not only make money but also cohere with the whole thrust of value investing. (Typically he would look for information that would signal whether a company was undervalued by the market.)
- Like other effective Idea Hunters, he has been happy to use other people's ideas. He might very well agree with Pablo Picasso, who is said to have remarked, "Good artists copy. Great artists steal."

Your Brain Is Open

Idea Hunters are interested in more than just a particular subject matter, or even a host of subject matters. It is hard to go very far with ideas unless you are also deeply interested in other people, especially in what they know and in their potential as collaborators.

Some of the most stellar performers, in business or other callings, were masterful because of the attention they paid to others. Miles Davis was one of the pacesetting trumpeters and band leaders in the jazz world, known widely for his virtuosity. But he defined himself chiefly by the company he kept, the people with whom he surrounded himself, and to whom he listened. As the saxophonist Wayne Shorter once said, "Miles wanted to play with people who knew more about music than he did. . . . He wasn't afraid of it." Even Miles Davis didn't think his musical brain was big enough to get all the ideas he wanted.

Paul Erdős was probably the most prolific mathematician of all time. An Eastern European émigré, he affixed his name to more scientific papers in the field than anyone else; he died in 1996 at age eighty-three. Mathematicians are by nature a solitary species, but Erdős traveled the planet in search of conversations about mathematical proofs, and was fond of declaring in his thick Hungarian accent, "My brain is open."

For most of his life, Erdős had no place to call home, no job to speak of, just a suitcase that could fit all his belongings. But he had an astounding 511 collaborators who coauthored most of his nearly 1,500 papers. He was so revered that mathematicians boasted of their Erdős Number, which represented their distance from the primary author of the papers. "Erdős # = 1" was the designation for those who collaborated directly with Erdős. Then there are those who have coauthored a paper with someone who coauthored a paper with the man himself—"Erdős # = 2." And so on.

Erdős made a point of remembering details about his collaborators, conversation partners, and hosts. "He knew everybody; what they were interested in; what they had conjectured, proved, or were in the midst of proving; their phone numbers; the names and ages of their wives, children, pets, and much more," writes biographer Bruce Schechter. "He could tell off the top of his head on which page in which obscure Russian journal a theorem similar to the one you were working on was proved in 1922. When he met a mathematician . . . he would immediately take up the conversation where they had left it two years earlier."

In other words, even for a mathematician as venerated as Erdős, idea work was not a solitary activity. It was unstintingly social. And he cultivated it.

All the same, the myth of the solitary genius dies hard. Perhaps no one embodied that myth—in the eyes of many—more surely than the master tinkerer, Thomas Edison. And it must be said that for a time, early in his career, Edison did try to work alone in his laboratory, free of encumbrances by other human minds. He set up a one-man lab in Boston, where he invented and patented an electric vote-counting machine. It was designed to instantly tally votes made by legislators at their desks in the statehouse.

The machine worked well enough—which was part of the problem. The legislators did not want their votes instantly tallied; they preferred to allow a bit of time between the initial casting and final counting of votes, so they could partake in last-minute lobbying and vote-trading. There was simply no market for this contraption.

The other part of the problem, with all of his work in Boston, was that Edison's brain wasn't wide open. He wasn't reaping the advantages of ideas batted around the laboratory floor by a broad mix of talented people. All that changed when he set up shop in New Jersey and cobbled together a team that included, among others, a German glassblower, an African-American engineer, a Swiss watchmaker, an American mathematician, and a British textile machinist. That is when he became the Edison we know and admire, the "wizard of Menlo Park."

At times Edison would backslide. He insisted, for example, on choosing by himself the music that he recorded in the fledgling days of the phonograph, an invention that Edison liked to call "my baby." As his great-grandniece, Sarah Miller Caldicott, relates (together with coauthor Michael Gelb) in *Innovate Like Edison*, one member of his team complained to Edison about his presumption. "A one-man opinion on tunes is all wrong," the wise associate said.

That was a small reversion to old habits, though. The story ends as Edison wins with ideas gained in collaboration with his team. Gelb and Caldicott point out that most of his competitors were introverts who dwelled on the technical aspects of their inventions, with little interest in the opinions of colleagues or potential customers. These inventors preferred "solitary and secret toil; they were either "incapable of team work, or jealous of any intrusion that could possibly bar them from a full and complete claim" to the final product or discovery, the authors write. "Edison always stood shoulder to shoulder with his associates, but no one questioned the leadership, nor was it ever in doubt where the inspiration originated."

All managers and professionals would do well to consider the power of "My brain is open." This begins with taking an active interest in the work of others, rather than being narrowly concerned with your own work. It means sharing your thoughts with colleagues, rather than keeping ideas under wraps and staying focused entirely on the job at hand. It also means encouraging ideas, not quashing them. For example, if you're a manager, and an employee walks up to you with an idea, you don't immediately say, "It won't fly." You say, "I'd like to hear more about it." As we'll see further in Chapter Six, it's important to send the right signals to idea-bearers. It's best to continue the conversation.

The right signals, good conversations, steady encouragement— these are essential, if the goal is to get ideas from people. And it should be, because no one person can squirrel away all the necessary notions. One of the most reliable ways of coming up with ideas is to make sure the people around us are coming up with ideas. Lots of them.

Defining Your Own Hunt

An Idea Hunter looks to other people for ideas, but also subscribes to Apple's motto: "Think different." Is there a contradiction here? Not really. The principal task is to step outside for ideas, to go beyond our own brains, because most of the ideas are elsewhere. But part of the challenge is to look for the kinds of ideas in the kinds of places that are likely to trigger something new and different. And that is why people need to take various paths in their search.

Our point is not that idea professionals should think like everybody else, or, conversely, should ignore everyone. It's that all professionals need to involve other people in their search for ideas. *And* they need to create their own map of The Hunt, which involves knowing your gig—what makes you different, among other things. The gig points your interest in certain directions, gives you a broad sense of what you need to learn, to achieve your goals. The work continues with decisions about the particular sources of information and ideas that constitute your map. Which ones are most likely to ramp up the value of a project you're working on? Which ones will contribute to a distinctive Hunt?

One story we're fond of telling is about the Norwegian explorer Roald Amundsen, who said, "There is no one so stupid that he does not have something sensible to say." He even looked upon dogs as "intelligent companions" in his perilous journey to the South Pole. He went to live among the Eskimos of Greenland, with the intent of learning all he could about their technologies, habits, and culture. He learned many valuable lessons, including the importance of maintaining a balanced diet while on expedition (to avoid vitamin deficiencies) and the need for ample rest and relaxation. He was deeply interested in what other people knew.

At the same time, he didn't listen only to what Europeans were saying about polar adventures, as most of his competitors did. Those sources were necessary—they included navigational experts, cartographers, and others—but not sufficient. They were not different and varied enough to produce the results he wanted; they were the same sources tapped by all the others in his field. And Amundsen was not going to let the other explorers define his Hunt, his search for ideas about how to win the Arctic challenge, the early-twentieth-century race to the South Pole. He went his own way, but not in a solitary way—he went toward people.

His interest in the customs of indigenous people was written off by many who saw these native inhabitants as "primitive" and "lazy." Some of his rivals tragically perished in the snow and ice, for lack of the knowledge that native communities had accumulated over centuries about how to survive long polar journeys. In 1911, Amundsen and his party became the first to reach the South Pole, largely because he defined his own Hunt.

Even in the safer precincts of New York or New Delhi, and almost everywhere in between, being interested can save your professional life. Almost by definition, interest means being interested in more than just a few things—and more than what people like you are saying and thinking. That is the challenge taken up more fully in the next chapter.

IDEAWORK #1

Selling the Best Hour of the Day to Yourself

Few people are accidental learners. For most of us, becoming an outstanding idea professional means putting time and effort into our thinking. It takes work and calls for conscious strategies. Here's one way to help make sure that happens: Carve out time every day for learning.

Charlie Munger hit upon one strategy when he was a young lawyer. He decided that whenever his legal work was not as intellectually stimulating as he'd like, "I would sell the best hour of the day to myself." He would take otherwise billable time at the peak of his day and dedicate it to his own thinking and learning. "And only after improving my mind—only after I'd used my best hour improving myself—would I sell my time to my professional clients. And I did that for a number of years," he said at the 2008 shareholders meeting of Wesco Financial, which he leads, and which is controlled by Warren Buffett's company, Berkshire Hathaway.

For both Munger and Buffett, reading and conversations are the basic stuff of daily learning time. Both of them have a preference for what Munger somewhat raffishly refers to as "ass time"—parts of the day when they're perusing published material at their desks.

Of course, not everyone can seal off a choice hour of office time every day for intellectual improvement. Even Munger said he would make an exception when a demanding situation arose. The important lessons here are that (1) learning is not something you do only when business is slow; (2) it is an intentional activity; and (3) everyone can make it a priority. Most managers and professionals would be able to run with some version of Munger's "sell the best hour" approach. Most would be able to deepen their knowledge, pursue their interests, and explore ideas on a daily basis.

Some companies have begun to institutionalize the notion of "sell the best hour." For example, 3M has long made it a practice to let employees set aside 20 percent of their time for work unrelated to the core business—in search of ideas and innovations.

Google follows the same drill. Most of its employees are allotted one day a week to follow their interests and passions. "This has produced more than a few of Google's technological breakthroughs. Just as important, it conveys a sense of freedom," writes Ken Auletta in his book *Googled: The End of the World as We Know It*, adding that the 20-percent rule also encourages engineers to "push the envelope, to assume that their mission is to disrupt traditional ways of doing things."

Marissa Mayer, who is Google's main overseer of product innovation, has said that half of the company's new products have stemmed from the 20-percent allotment. One example is Google News, the automated news aggregator that premiered in 2006. (Google has other ways of nurturing the thinking and conversation behind the innovations. For instance, borrowing an idea from university life, Mayer holds open office hours three times a week, welcoming all those who have a notion they'd like to entertain.) Copying 3M and Google, a slew of other companies, including Intuit and Facebook, are now offering 20-percent time as well.

At W. L. Gore, a half-day of every employee's week is turned over to "dabble time" for projects entirely of their choosing. The company is best known for its breathable waterproof fabric GORE-TEX, which is used in many kinds of sportswear. But Gore has also developed such wildly varied products as dental floss, cardiac implants, and industrial gaskets and hoses. "At its core, Gore is a marketplace of ideas," observes Gary Hamel in his book *The Future of Management.* The discretionary time enjoyed by employees has served as the main fuel for this innovation machine.

One of the more spectacular fruits of dabble time is the company's line of guitar strings, which keep their tone several times longer than other guitar strings. This is achieved by virtue of a special coating that was developed from a Gore effort to improve push-pull cables. Elixir Strings, originally a dabble-time project, has now cornered the U.S. market for guitar strings.

What all this shows is that breakthroughs happen when people attend to their professional curiosities and set aside time for deliberate learning. Dabble time is not wasted time. It is a seedbed of innovation, a habit that expands the store of knowledge.

With or without a formal company policy, every individual professional can make time for learning or experimentation, even during the work day. It could be a matter of what you do with the half-hour before you get going in the morning or during lunch. Do you check in on blogs, scan the *New York Times*, jot down some wild ideas? Are there any particular web sites that seem to be most deserving of your self-improvement time?

Another avenue is to spend core work hours more deliberately—with an eye toward ideas and knowledge. What kinds of questions are you asking at meetings? What sorts of conversations are you pursuing in the hallways? What are you noticing when you visit a client or come in contact with a customer? How will your work on the project today add to what you know, not just what you do? Henry David Thoreau put it this way: "It's not enough to be busy. So are the ants. The question is: What are we busy about?" Everyone today should be busy about learning new things and seeking out ideas.

Andy usually starts off his seminars with an exercise. Each participant is asked to spend fifteen minutes talking to at least four people in the group—not for the purpose of finding out what their favorite dishes or hobbies are, but for purposes of the Hunt. Each one is asked to learn something that is valuable to him or her professionally. When the time is up, Andy puts a series of questions to the group. *How many learned something of real value, something that is likely to improve your work?* Invariably about 90 percent of the hands go up. *Would you have learned much of anything if you were simply making introductions, as is normally done at the start of a seminar?* The consensus is always "No." *So why did you learn?* Usually at least a couple of people answer immediately: "Because you told us to."

Finally, the seminar participants are asked what extra time was involved in getting the new idea(s) during this learning. And the answer is "None." In a typical seminar, they would have spent around fifteen minutes getting to know each other anyway. The difference is that they used the time deliberately to search for knowledge and ideas. And they took the first step, which is to be interested.

Whether you're carving out new time or learning more intently in the course of regular work, the key is to somehow become liberated from the routine. Too often, the normal procedure is to stay narrowly focused on doing the work, rather than on learning what's needed to improve the work. Most professionals today understand that they need to invest in themselves. One way of doing so is to, literally or otherwise, sell a productive hour of the day to yourself, for continued learning.

I
Diverse
E
A

CHAPTER 3

Diversifying
the Hunt

JIM KOCH IS THE FOUNDER and chairman of the Boston
Beer Company, best known for its flagship brand, Samuel Adams
Boston Lager. He recalls that in his former career as a management
consultant in Boston, he seldom thought explicitly about how and
where to find ideas. As a consequence, he did not come up with
very many of them, in his estimation. That changed, however, in
the early 1980s, when Koch decided to strike out on his own and
explore entrepreneurial possibilities. Suddenly the ideas started bub-
bling up around him. Why? Because he was looking for them.

"My sense was that once I started looking for business ideas,
they were everywhere," he told us in an interview. "It's sort of like
radio frequency. You're surrounded by radio waves, but if you're not
tuning into them, you're not going to receive them."

Koch's revelation, of course, was that he needed to go looking.
But he also realized that he would have to search in many different
places, because ideas are all over the map. We will return to his Hunt
and how it led to Boston Beer in a moment. For now the key point
is that those who want to find exceptional ideas need to travel down
a variety of paths. And the key word here is "diverse"—the second
of the I-D-E-A principles introduced in this book. Diversity is one

way of sharpening your personal brand, distinguishing what you have to offer from what other people have to offer. You have to be different in some positive way if you want to make a difference in an organization. And part of being different is to get new ideas from a wide mix of sources, not just in all the usual places.

Unlikely sources were of interest to Thomas Edison, who remarked on more than one occasion, "Ah, Shakespeare. That's where you get the ideas!" What could he have meant by this?

We do not know if Edison's pursuit of the incandescent light bulb was somehow inspired by King Claudius's command in *Hamlet*, "Give me some light!" We have no idea if his thinking about the phonograph was influenced by the mysterious noises that enthralled Caliban in *The Tempest*. But his admiration for the Bard, and in particular Shakespeare's use of metaphor and analogy (as in *Richard III*: "Now is the winter of our discontent"), was well known. Edison believed that the ability to see analogies was the key to invention. For example, he looked at the way messages flow through telegraph equipment and conceptualized an analogous flow of electricity through wires and filaments. That was part of his musing about the light bulb, as Michael Gelb and Sarah Miller Caldicott note in *Innovate Like Edison*.

More to the point, Edison believed that the best learning was diverse learning, and he wanted all of his collaborators to know a lot of different things. All prospective employees had to take a written test of 150 questions geared toward different jobs and classifications of workers. College graduates were asked a bracing spectrum of questions such as: "What is the first line in the *Aeneid*? Who composed *Il Trovatore*? What voltage is used on streetcars?" Cabinet makers were asked: "Which countries supply the most mahogany? Who was the Roman emperor when Jesus Christ was born?" Edison is said to have demanded scores of 90 percent or better for anyone to qualify for initiation into what became known as his "Invention Factory." The message was that people need to think broadly and creatively no matter what job they're doing; an engineer can learn a thing or two from Shakespeare.

There is a store of traditional wisdom behind such thinking, and no small amount of modern empirical research. The eighteenth-century philosopher Adam Smith observed, "When the mind is employed about a variety of objects, it is somehow expanded and enlarged." He was referring generally to the traits of people who built the commercial systems during the early stages of capitalism. Another towering figure of early modern thought was the philosopher John Stuart Mill, whose writings on liberty continue to inform politics and economics today. "It is hardly possible to overrate the value . . . of placing human beings in contact with persons dissimilar to themselves, and with modes of thought and action unlike those with which they are familiar," he said. "Such communication has always been, and is peculiarly in the present age, one of the primary sources of progress."

The Color of Your Ideas

That is diversity as we see it. And then there's "diversity" in the multicultural sense—representation along the lines of group identity. The key markers tend to be gender, race, and ethnicity; increasingly other factors, such as educational and professional background and age, are figuring into the picture. This is not our particular focus: we are interested primarily in the color of one's ideas, the breadth of sources that spawn innovation. But we want to briefly draw a link between the Idea Hunt and diversity in that second sense, as it is understood in most organizations.

In the end, what is the added business value of diversity as commonly understood? It derives from the simple fact that people have different backgrounds and experiences, and these differences can produce a lively flow of ideas. Indeed, a growing body of research has found that diverse workforces contribute measurably to performance. For example, the global consulting firm Accenture has conducted a long-running study that compares companies with diverse executive boards to those that are more uniform. The study finds that diverse boards, by a range of measures including profitability, tend to be more successful than others.

We live in a time of increasing complexity. Executives at high levels of management need to "understand, embrace, and act on an amalgam of viewpoints, constantly questioning established ways of doing things and providing an antidote to the groupthink that stymies innovation," Accenture explained in a summer 2010 report. Management teams are more likely to do so if their members include men and women with different areas of expertise and knowledge and who come from different ethnic and racial groups. In addition, the report specifically pointed out the need to involve younger managers in the mix. There should be a balance between what Accenture described as "the graybeards and the greenhorns" (the latter meaning the younger managers).

It's not hard to see how a lack of diversity along those lines could choke the flow of fresh thinking. An alarming case in point was the 2008 meltdown of the financial industry. Wall Street is (in)famously populated by men from top to bottom, among them a disproportionate number of young male traders—far too many "greenhorns" in this case. Risk-taking, stubbornness, and aggression—often tagged as typically male traits—probably helped produce the flush times during the run-up to the financial crisis. But the same tendencies, when unchecked, also proved disastrous at a moment when financial professionals needed to be more cautious than greedy. They needed to admit that they were going in the wrong direction and that it was time to explore alternative paths.

As one female financial manager put it, "If there's a position going sour on me, I'm not going to sit and say, 'I know what's best.' It would make me want to raise my hand and get advice from other people. It's like asking for directions when driving." Nancy Davis of Goldman Sachs made this comment in a *New York Magazine* article provocatively titled, "What If Women Ran Wall Street?" by Sheelah Kolhatkar. Another analyst, referring to the financial crackup and the preponderance of males in that sector, explained, "It was like herd behavior. They all think the same, they're all from the same school, with the same friends, the same jargon, the same books. You get very unbalanced as a consequence." The upshot: not enough people were of a mind to ask questions and go looking for fresh ideas. There was a price to be paid for this sameness.

Ideas are like personnel. You need different kinds to boost performance and get the job done. You need ideas from outside your specialty—and people of differing skills and talents. The best ideas (or employees) are not found by looking in just one place or where everyone else is looking. That's not the way to find ideas (or teams) that will help you and your organization stand out.

Appreciating the value of diversity is a good start for the Idea Hunter. The next move is to think more about the people with whom you normally converse and from whom you get your notions. How diverse a group are they, in terms of what they know and how they think?

When Weak Ties Are Strong

Decades of statistical research have demonstrated that professionals need to think elastically about the people in their idea networks.

For example, repeated studies have shown that the longer a project team stays together without significant changes in its composition, the less likely it is to come up with ideas that lead to innovations. This is largely because members of long-running teams get into the habit of culling their ideas from a narrow band of sources: one another. They're less likely to communicate with people working on other projects and in other departments, and professionally through other channels outside the organization. They're less likely to come up with fresh solutions to problems.

People on your team would fall into the category of "strong ties," meaning that you and they belong to overlapping networks of information and ideas. Someone in a different specialty altogether would count as a "weak tie," as this person normally travels in a different set of circles organizationally or professionally. Part of achieving real diversity is to understand "The Strength of Weak Ties," which is the title of a 1973 paper by the American sociologist Mark Granovetter.

Granovetter laid out a seminal social-networking theory that remains highly influential today. He showed that the most valuable information comes from outside a person's usual network of contacts, through weak ties. He based his finding on interviews with hundreds of job seekers. They were far more likely to land a job through a "weak" acquaintance than through a friend, relative, or coworker with whom they shared the same connections. The strong-tie contacts ordinarily spoke to roughly the same people that the job seekers spoke to, so they had more or less the same leads to offer.

In professional life, some of the best ideas will come from weak-tie individuals, whose conversational networks are different from ours. They may well have an entirely different perspective on a subject, one that expands our supply of knowledge and ideas.

People like that are very important to Idea Hunters. They are customers, acquaintances, and many others—including perfect strangers. They do not fit easily into conventional notions of where and from whom to get "expert" opinions, because they're not experts. That's not their function. Their role is to say things you might not otherwise hear, spark thoughts that otherwise might not come to mind. What they provide is not a substitute for expertise; it is a supplement.

For example, if you're getting into the beer business, you'll naturally want to learn from beer distributors, wholesalers, marketers, and others in the know. But don't forget to talk to the guy sitting on the barstool next to you.

That's what Jim Koch did one day in 1984 after walking into a bar at Faneuil Hall in Boston. "I was doing market research," Koch recalled—with a laugh, because he had really walked into the establishment in need of a drink. But his thirst did not stand in the way of his Hunt. At the time he was already toying with the notion of starting a small craft brewery—his family had been in the business for a few generations. And so he grabbed a stool and began tuning in to his surroundings. He struck up a conversation with a fellow who was holding a Heineken and asked him why he was drinking that particular brew. "I like imported beer," the man replied. Then Koch asked him how he liked the taste, and the response was surprising, given his stated preference for imported brands. "It tastes skunky," was the response.

"Skunky" is a beer term for spoiled. At least at the time, imported beers did not have a fresh taste, only in part because they had to travel long distances to the United States. Most of the imported brands also came in clear or green bottles. (They still do, for marketing appeal.) But it was a problem, because hops—the key ingredient—spoils with exposure to light. That is why beer has traditionally come in darker-colored bottles, which shield the light-sensitive hops.

It was not a problem, though, for Koch. It was an incredible opportunity. He describes the conversation at Faneuil Hall as his "wow" moment when he realized that he could succeed in the high-end beer market with a fresh-tasting beer. In other words, he could take on the imports, which accounted for just 5 percent of the American beer market at that time. "Their whole business model was based on selling stale and skunky beer to Americans and trying to cover it up with this old-world imagery," Koch told us. (As for the domestic brands, they too were often stale by the time they reached consumers, at least partly because they spent too much time in warehouses.)

The stranger at Faneuil Hall (a "weak-tie" contact) was a case in point. Evidently he was drinking Heineken for the image and prestige, even while thinking it had a spoiled taste. Talking to that man in that place, not to a wholesaler in a warehouse, was the spark of insight for Koch. He still had much to do along the way to developing his high-end product and carving out a market for it. And he would have to educate the public on the basic fact that beer is a highly perishable product. But he was well on his way. A year after the barroom conversation, Koch launched the Boston Beer Company, which is now by far the largest craft brewery in the United States.

Widening Your Intellectual Bandwidth

Koch used the image of radio frequencies. We draw on another broadcasting analogy, "bandwidth"—the breadth of information and knowledge to which we are receptive. Breadth matters. An Internet technology manager can certainly find good ideas by reading a publication like *Information Technology News*—in fact, it's must reading for anyone in the field. The problem is that almost everyone *else* in the field reads it too. There are other places to go for ideas that might help distinguish one manager's projects from another. If you're that manager, you don't gain an edge simply by talking to other tech people, who generally know what you know. You do so by fashioning an extended web of knowledge, a robust range of sources, which will help you to steer clear of the me-too ideas that come from operating within a narrow bandwidth. That's the way to avoid bad *breadth*.

When we think of intellectual bandwidth, our thoughts turn to a number of people. Among them is someone not very well known in the business world: Jack Hughes, founder and chairman of Top-Coder, a global software company launched in 2000. TopCoder has pioneered the model of "crowdsourcing" in that industry, creating a community of (at last count) 250,000 freelance software developers around the world. They do all the software coding, which provides solutions to clients ranging from AOL and Best Buy to GEICO and the Royal Bank of Scotland.

To be sure, Hughes and his team stay on top of technical developments in their field. But they are emphatic about the need to look for business ideas elsewhere. Referring to the software industry, he told us, "I almost never look to the existing discipline for new ideas. Most of the time, I actively avoid it. I'm not sure why, but if I had to guess, I'd have to say that I want to avoid it coloring my thinking and setting me down the wrong path. So I look to other disciplines—manufacturing, the arts, science, finance, etc."

And sports. An avid college basketball fan, Hughes examined the tournament structure of the National Collegiate Athletic Association and applied that structure to software competitions held by TopCoder. This is the modus operandi of the company. Members of the community take part in contests to come up with creative designs and solutions, and they are rewarded handsomely for the best work.

As a way of generating excitement, Hughes looked to the NCAA's "March Madness" basketball tournaments, in which the season rises to a crescendo through multiple playoff rounds, culminating in a championship. TopCoder's main tournament begins with up to eight thousand entrants and is whittled down to about two hundred through elimination rounds. (More often than not, the programmers do these jobs in their spare time, although the ones who devote their full time to the company crank out most of the work.)

TopCoder also developed a ratings system for programmers. This is primarily for their benefit: the coders use these ratings as a way of deciding which competitions they should enter. They base their decisions in part on the scores of other programmers taking on the challenges, which indicate their chances of winning. In devising this system, Hughes and his managers turned to the world of chess, and in particular to the rankings of grandmaster chess players who take part in world competition. So, like elite chess players, the highest-rated programmers receive a "red rating" while coders at other levels are given other colors.

In the meantime, Hughes kept widening his intellectual bandwidth. He began to pay close attention to a recent development in Major League Baseball statistics: the proliferation of new metrics for player performance that go far beyond the traditional RBI's and so forth. Talk of baseball stats got the people at TopCoder thinking about the breadth of ratings they use for programmers. "People aren't just interested in a [single] rating as they are in an SAT score. They're also interested in the stats that make them up. How many at bats? How many hits and runs, etc.," Hughes said, explaining how he began to analogize from baseball. With that in mind, the coders were given different statistics relating to the number of competitions they entered, their highest and lowest scores, and their averages, among other metrics. The company went so far as to post electronic "baseball cards" for each programmer—with box scores featuring the various coding statistics.

For coders, the ratings system is itself a big part of the attraction to this professional community. It provides a way of objectively assessing their ability and establishing a record of their performance. A 2010 case study published by *Harvard Business Review* pointed out that many prestigious software firms now ask prospective employees to "get a TopCoder rating" before applying for a job.

Referring to parallels like baseball statistics, Hughes said, "We watch this stuff like hawks. We're always looking for analogies. We're looking for analogs that have a high rate of affinity for what we're working on." Hughes is in good company on this score, as we saw earlier in the example of Thomas Edison's analogical imagination. To analogize is to "recognize a correspondence of inner relationship or of function between two or more different phenomenon or complex sets of phenomena," according to a definition by Robert and Michele Root-Bernstein, a physiologist and artist, respectively. They include analogizing among their "13 Thinking Tools" for creativity and innovation; among other tools cited are observing, synthesizing, and empathizing.

Analogies from other worlds have helped TopCoder forge a new way of developing software, as well as the first rating system for programmers. That system not only serves a practical function but, with its baseball cards and chess colors, has also added to the buzz surrounding this innovative organization. Little of this would have happened if Hughes and his company were operating within a narrow bandwidth, within the confines of one specialty. They innovated because they were looking to see how the world out there connects with their plans and projects.

Hughes noted, "We are experts in software, but we're not going to learn a lot" from other software developers about gaining an edge in this business. "There's a parochialism among experts that sort of blinds them to what could be," he explained. "We want diversity."

Bridging Distant Worlds

Diversity makes it possible to span distances: between your brain and other brains, your specialty and other specialties, your world and other worlds. Between baseball and software—or taxis and Twitter.

The social networking site has its conceptual roots in an altogether different sphere. The company's creator, Jack Dorsey, had a fascination with cities and their inner workings, especially the way people, vehicles, and packages move around a metropolis. This inspired him to develop software tracking the whereabouts, via the Internet, of bicycles and trucks that were en route delivering packages. In 2000, barely into his mid-twenties, Dorsey was running a dispatching business in Oakland, California, as he explained in a 2009 *Los Angeles Times* interview with David Sarno.

> Then we started adding in the next element, which are taxi cabs. Now we have another entity roaming about the metropolis, reporting what it is and what work it has, going over CPS or CB radio or cell phone. And then you get to the emergency services: ambulances, fire trucks, and police—and suddenly you have this very rich sense of what's happening right now in the city.
>
> But it's missing the public. It's missing normal people.
> That's where Twitter came in . . .
> This aspect where you can just locate your buddy list and at a glance locate what your friends are up to, or what they say they're up to. I found the same parallels in dispatch—here's a bunch of ambulances and couriers reporting where they are, and here's my friends.

Dorsey launched Twitter in 2006 together with Biz Stone and Evan Williams. In doing so, they bridged two worlds—vehicle dispatching and social networking. They spanned the distance between two familiar realms and spawned an innovation. In this case, unlike Jack Hughes and the baseball statistics, Dorsey didn't have to step into another world in order to learn about dispatching and courier services. He was already in that business. But he used the basic ideas of that business and extended them into the realm of social networking. Out of that melding came a whole new service. And it all began with Dorsey's interest in different kinds of ideas drawn from different settings, which is the hallmark of a diverse Idea Hunt.

Edison was a master of such melding. Andrew Hargadon of the University of California, Davis, has closely studied the inventor's methods and his idea factory in Menlo Park, New Jersey. A noted expert in technology management, Hargadon points out that people in the Edison laboratory took their knowledge of electromagnetic power from the telegraph industry, where most of them had worked, and transferred the old ideas to products they developed for other industries, such as mining and railways. In other words, old ideas suddenly became new.

Edison and his team knew there are really two products of work: what you make and what you learn in the process. And your learning is more diverse if you're working on different products for different sectors and industries. Occupying such a spectrum of spaces, the technicians in the Edison lab picked up knowledge they couldn't have gained by working in a single industry. They bridged "distant worlds," in Hargadon's words. As he points out, the phonograph blended old ideas from products that Edison's engineers (and others) had developed for the telegraph, telephone, and electric motor industries. Hargadon's understated conclusion: "Edison's inventions were not wholly original. Like most creative acts and products, they were extensions and blends of existing knowledge."

Bridging distant worlds may sound like a feat accomplished by those at a far higher pay grade than most of us. And it is true that some very illustrious people have come up with extraordinary products by making such connections. But it is important to remember that ideas are already out there. No part of this process requires an act of creative genius.

Recall Phil Schiller and the Apple team that produced the iPod. They were casting about for the right user interface for their new music player and found what they needed in a motley collection of electronics, among them the Hewlett Packard 9836 Workstation. Introduced in 1983, this computer had a keyboard with a wheel for scrolling text, similar to what became the click wheel of iPods (not including touchscreen versions). Schiller bridged the distance between one product and another that he was trying to improve (music players).

The click wheel was an old idea, waiting to be dusted off and put to some other use. It wasn't an invention. And here again we bump up against that myth that needs to be exposed—the belief that invention is the source of all innovation, that the only great idea is a thoroughly original one. This myth can lure people away from potentially valuable ideas that already exist, often in a mundane form (like components of a telephone, in the case of Edison and the phonograph), and it can send them off on a maddening search for that elusive goal: pure originality. This was not how Edison worked. Any originality in his approach consisted of his willingness to go looking for ideas in an interesting range of settings and then combine them into something new. He usually succeeded by "rubbing two ideas together," to borrow a phrase from one of Andy's old professors.

Consider a celebrated example of such an "invention." The Reebok Pump was one of the iconic technologies of the 1990s and has become a footwear classic. It was the first line of running shoes to feature an inflatable bladder that allows for customized fitting and exceptional comfort. The principal agent of this innovation was

Design Continuum, Inc., a Boston-area firm that has developed products ranging from squirt guns and surgical devices to nursery monitors and inline skates.

One might think that the principals of Design Continuum would be quick to take credit as the "inventors" of the Reebok Pump. But that's not how they look at things. "It was innovative, it wasn't invention. And we knew that we didn't have to invent anything," one Design Continuum manager told Hargadon, who is himself a former design engineer. "We knew you could call up this company and get little check valves and call up this company and get little molded rubber parts and on and on. And these welded things, all these things that the shoe industry had no connection to." Having worked on hospital equipment, the designers also knew they could call up a manufacturer of intravenous feeding bags to get the basic technology for the air bladders.

The team members were able to do all this because of the breadth of their ties to many products and industries, which broadened their knowledge and offered a rich collection of ideas. The instructive irony is that they had a better perspective on producing a running shoe than the shoe experts did. Diversity proved more valuable than expertise. If Design Continuum engineers had devoted their efforts to studying the ins and outs of existing shoe technology, they probably wouldn't have come up with the Pump. As Hargadon points out—again, in his illuminating study *How Breakthroughs Happen*—the entire design project wound up costing $250,000. In the first year the Reebok Pump was introduced, it brought in more than $1 billion.

Ideas Are Everywhere

We started this chapter by relating Jim Koch's recollection that once he started looking for business ideas, they seemed to be everywhere. There's a slightly different way of constructing this: if you believe that ideas are everywhere, then you'll start finding them in droves. Such was the spirit that Jack Welch brought to American business, particularly to General Electric, in the 1980s. Until then, corporate America shared an animus against any idea or product "not invented here," placing an exclusive priority on the creation of novel ideas within the boundaries of an organization. People were rewarded with bonuses to the extent that they conjured up such notions.

Welch arrived on the scene and set out a new vision. He originally called it "integrated diversity," but the approach came to be known, more felicitously, as "boundarylessness." "For our entire history, we had rewarded the inventor or the person who came up with a good idea," he later wrote in his 2001 book *Jack: Straight from the Gut*. "Boundarylessness would make heroes out of people who recognized and developed a good idea, not just those who came up with one." One result: leaders were encouraged to share the credit with their teams rather than take full credit themselves. Another result: GE went looking for ideas in the wide corporate world— "Someone, somewhere has a better idea," he said—and happily adapted these ideas to its specific needs. As Welch once commented in a documentary, "It's a badge of honor to have found from Motorola a quality program, from HP a product development program, from Toyota an asset management system."

This is an extremely important attitude for an Idea Hunter. Trying to come up with thoroughly original ideas all the time (to the extent that any useful ideas exist completely within the confines of a single brain) is a losing game. The better plan is to identify potentially valuable ideas that either are already being used or have been used in the past. The task then is to slip those ideas into your setting or circumstances.

We spoke earlier about Jack Hughes of TopCoder, who transported ideas from baseball statistics and other distant realms to his software enterprise. "Almost everything I do is borrowed and repurposed from others in other fields," he recapped in an e-mail note after our visit to his offices in Connecticut. "I look at myself as an innovator. Innovation is different than original thinking. Original thinkers are very rare. They are able to tease out the inner workings of nature, often overturning entrenched dogma in the process. I would reserve this distinction for some of the greatest scientists and mathematicians." The rest of us don't need to dwell on whether we're coming up with original ideas. No less a creative figure than Twyla Tharp, the acclaimed American dancer and choreographer, has made this exact point. "Personally, I don't worry about originality at all," she told the *Harvard Business Review* in 2008. "Has anyone ever done what I've done before? Yeah, probably. But I'm not going to worry about it; I'm going to use it and get on with it."

Innovation is fueled by diversity. And part of a diverse game plan is to take ideas in one setting and use them in a very different one, as Hughes did with the baseball metrics. This is where repurposing (referred to in Chapter One) reenters the picture. Here we'd like to stress a particular point: People repurpose all the time, in their ordinary activities. They enjoy a dinner of steak, peppers, and onions at a restaurant and decide they're going to incorporate those ingredients into a pasta dish they make at home. They see an old dresser in the attic and think they'll use it to store stuff in the garage. Very often, a casual idea will spill over into work. Someone might read a concise, informative, three-hundred-word article in the local paper, and the next morning she'll be adapting that style for a business memo.

People do all that and more, without thinking twice. And that's fine, for recreational cooking and yard work and the like. But finding high-value ideas is serious business for those who want to reach peak performance in today's hypercompetitive professional markets. It pays, therefore, to be deliberate and intentional about the search for ideas. It's important to condition yourself for a daily Idea Hunt, which is the focus of Chapter Four.

IDEAWORK #2
The I's and T's

Idea hunters have wide intellectual *bandwidth.* Seeking out knowledge in a flexible array of settings is part and parcel of their innovation plan. What does this say about how a professional develops his or her skill set and knowledge base? More specifically, is it a disadvantage today to be a hard-core specialist—someone who looks for knowledge through a fairly narrow lens? Should everyone be a generalist?

Here it is useful to think about two kinds—or shapes—of professionals. One can be shaped either like an "I" (think narrow and tight) or a "T" (think extended). The *I*-shaped professional is highly versed in a specific area of expertise and learns by drilling more deeply into a particular field. The *T*-shaped person has broader skills and knowledge and learns by linking up different perspectives from different specialties. (This terminology apparently originated at McKinsey & Company in internal conversations about what kinds of consultants to hire.)

Both types are essential in any organization. Many leaders today, however, feel that *T* people are better at fostering the diverse connections and conversations that bring exceptional ideas to the surface. And they bemoan what they see as a dearth of them in today's hyperspecialized environments. Recently, Bill was talking to the head of research and development at a major global communications company. The person said, "We have a lot of *I*'s. What we need are more *T*'s."

For us, the issue is not whether it is better to be an *I* or a *T.* That is an involved question, touching on the many different kinds of work that need to be done in an organization and a given person's choice of career or calling. But regardless of the role you play in your organization, you need to develop at least some *T* characteristics. You have to set your mind to broadening your sources of information and knowledge in order to get better ideas for your projects.

Consider Warren Buffett. He would have to be considered an *I* person in the sense that his gig (what he's all about as a professional) is tightly focused on finding better ways to invest money. As biographer Roger Lowenstein notes, "His talent lay not in his range—which was narrowly focused on investing—but in his intensity." True, but he did make a point of seeking out sources of ideas that were unfrequented by other investors. Most of his colleagues were primarily interested in the mechanics of the stock market. Buffett, however, searched for information about the intrinsic value of a given company. Rather than limit his idea search to a narrow cluster of familiar sources, he cast his net more widely than the competition did.

In 1963, Buffett was closely studying American Express. At the time, the company boasted a million cardholders, but things soon began to unravel. A New Jersey subsidiary of the company imploded in a scandal involving fraud (by a third party), and American Express stock plunged by nearly 50 percent. In the midst of this crisis, Buffett continued to study the company—but in unusual ways.

He went to a place called Ross's Steak House in Omaha, where his chief purpose was not to chow down but to sit near the cashier and talk to the owner. He observed that patrons were still using American

Express cards to pay for their dinners, and he assumed that the same would be true in other cities.

The next day, he dropped in on banks and travel agencies that use American Express traveler's checks. And then he turned up at supermarkets and drug stores where he had seen customers purchasing the company's money orders. On all counts, the American Express trade was brisk. Buffett also spoke to the company's competitors. As Lowenstein summarizes:

> His sleuthing led to two conclusions, both at odds with prevailing wisdom:
>
> 1. American Express was not going down the tubes.
> 2. Its name was one of the great franchises in the world.

As investors grew ever more fearful of American Express stock, Buffett became greedy. He put nearly a quarter of his assets into the stock. Sure enough, American Express's value began to rise again on Wall Street. (We should point out that it wasn't Buffett's purchasing that drove the value up; this was back in the days before his actions became so closely followed and emulated that they could power market movements.) Throughout this particular Hunt for ideas, Buffett remained fixated on one question: Should I invest in American Express? That question was part of his gig as an I professional who was concerned almost exclusively with finding better ways to invest. Nevertheless, he didn't put himself where all the other investors were; he didn't just read the usual distilled reports by stock analysts or stare at the ticker tape. Rather, he extended himself into diverse settings—places where few, if any, investors were trolling for ideas. In this way he took on the broad shape of a *T* while still staying obsessively, narrowly, singularly focused.

All this is another way of saying that there's nothing wrong with being a card-carrying *I* as long as you can also be a *T* in some significant sense. You could do the most specialized work in the world and still benefit greatly from wide intellectual bandwidth, from the insights that can be gleaned from almost anywhere. You could be an investor and yet find valuable ideas at a grocery store.

Most professionals today have an area of specialization, but they are more likely to find distinctive ideas if they have one foot outside their "small worlds"—a term used by Andrew Hargadon to describe immediate professional contexts, such as a specialty or industrial sector.

There are two ways of extending beyond a specialized world, and they both run in similar directions. One way, of course, is to become something of a generalist. You could focus primarily on broadening rather than deepening what you know, perhaps by pursuing projects that would involve diverse sets of clients and collaborators. The second way, which is equally effective, is to stay close to your specialty but work on developing closer ties to people outside that area. These people can be *T*'s or specialists in other fields. They're the ones who get us beyond what former Intel strategist Cindy Rabe refers to as "ExpertThink"—the professional bubble in which everyone thinks and does as we do.

Either way, you're expanding your perspective, encountering ideas from sources that may elude others. You're becoming more of a *T*. All you need is a willingness to extend yourself into different and unfamiliar areas of knowledge and practice, into your discomfort zones. That's where the "wow" ideas are.

I

D

Exercised

A

CHAPTER 4

Mastering the Habits of the Hunt

WE HAVE BOTH SPENT TIME AS TEACHERS and consultants in Lausanne, Switzerland, home of the International Olympic Committee. Each year, most countries send delegations to the IOC to confer about rules or discuss where to hold future events, and these contingents almost always include some world-class athletes. It's easy to recognize the famous ones as they jog or sprint along Lake Geneva in the early morning hours, making their way through the vineyards of surrounding villages. Their intensity, focus, and commitment are almost palpable. Even during a noncompetitive junket to Switzerland, the Olympians put serious time into exercising. They realize that their success as athletes, their fortunes and reputations, turn on the ability to perform better than their competition.

Much the same can be said about managers and other professionals. They need to spend time mentally working out—exercising their idea muscles. This is the third of the I-D-E-A principles. And when we speak of exercise, we are not touting the benefits of brain teasers, like the games that have become popular motivational tools in business—recognizing shapes, finding hidden words, and other mind benders. "Accomplished people don't bulk up their brains with intellectual calisthenics; they immerse themselves in their fields," explains Steven Pinker, a cognitive scientist at Harvard University. "Novelists read lots of novels, scientists read lots of science."

We would go further and say that people who excel at the Hunt immerse themselves both inside and outside their fields. Furthermore, they don't wait for an acute problem to arise before beginning their search for ideas, and their Hunt is not confined to the occasional conference or monthly brainstorming session. They are searching habitually and continually.

Sam Walton searched that way. The retail giant's former COO, Don Soderquist, tells of the *second* time he met Walton. The first time, in 1964, was in Chicago, at a business meeting. Soderquist was in charge of data processing at Ben Franklin, a chain of retail stores owned by individual proprietors and franchised by the company. Walton was a franchisee (in addition to having opened his first Wal-Mart store, two years earlier, in Arkansas). The meeting was fairly routine, but Soderquist's next encounter with Walton was not.

> The next day was Saturday, and I went shopping, dressed in a pair of mangy cutoff jeans—at the Kmart near my house. I walked over into the apparel section and saw this guy talking to one of the clerks. I thought, "Jeez, that looks like that guy I met yesterday. What the heck is he doing way out here?" I strolled up behind him, and I could hear him asking this clerk, "Well, how frequently do you order? . . . Uh-huh. . . . How much do you order?" . . . He's writing everything she says down in a little blue spiral notebook. Then Sam gets down on his hands and knees and he's looking under this stack table, and he opens the sliding doors and says, "How do you know how much you've got under here when you're placing that order?"

Finally, I said, "Sam Walton, is that you?" And he looked up from the floor and said, "Oh, Don! Hi! What are you doing here?" I said, "I'm shopping. What are *you* doing?" And he said, "Oh, this is just part of the educational process. That's all."

Walton made a habit of prowling for ideas in other people's stores, as he relates in his 1992 autobiography *Sam Walton, Made in America*. It was "just part of the educational process," part of his regular exercise. And it continued throughout his life, though there came a time when the blue spiral notebook was supplanted by a tape recorder. Walton had the right attitude as an Idea Hunter. "You can learn from everybody," he taught. "I probably learned the most by studying what my competitor was doing across the street." He gladly conceded that all the ideas tried at Wal-Mart, such as how and where to display items, were copied from other stores. His wife, Helen, says he seemed to spend almost as much time in other people's stores as he did in his own.

The Practice of Ideas

When Walton was nosing around a competitor's store, he was not doing pointless mental calisthenics. He was in the game, getting real ideas. That is the principal way of exercising idea muscles. Aristotle said, "What we have to learn to do, we learn by doing." We practice idea work in the same general sense that a physician practices medicine—by doing it. We pick up the habits of the Hunt by digging for ideas consciously and systematically.

What should be added to Aristotle's dictum (and in harmony with his thinking) is that people also learn by *reflecting* on what they're doing. In other words, part of the task is to regularly take stock of your progress as an Idea Hunter. This could be as simple as asking yourself questions at the end of the week. What's my daily "educational process"? Did I read a newspaper in the past few days? Did I take part in any stimulating conversations? What have I learned this week? Did I make connections between my personal experiences and my projects? Did I run any ideas by other people?

Exercise is indispensable because ideas come to those who are in the habit of looking for ideas. There is, however, a lingering sense among many that ideas really come to those who are uniquely creative; or perhaps they arrive out of the blue, with little prompting or preparation. There are kernels of truth in both of these beliefs, but they tend to ignore the stories of remarkable Idea Hunters, people like Sam Walton, whose success had more to do with his search for ideas than with his degree of creative genius. When it comes to the Hunt, behavior counts more than brilliance.

It's true that an idea can surface when you least suspect it, popping into your head when you're gardening on a Saturday morning or tearing into a chicken salad wrap. But keep in mind that serendipity of this sort is not unrelated to your practice as an idea professional. Why does the idea come to mind, and why are you able to recognize and understand its potential?

Louis Pasteur, the French scientist who invented pasteurization, pointed out, "Chance favors the prepared mind." His point was about the habits of research that usually lie behind any scientific discovery, however serendipitous. Someone who develops those skills is more likely than others to create his or her own luck in the search for breakthroughs. For Sir Isaac Newton, seeing the apple fall to the ground (if not directly on his head, as legend has it) was a chance occurrence. But he was not the first scientist to see such an event. The falling apple sparked his insights about the laws of motion because he had done his homework and always kept an eye out for discovery. Newton was in shape for the Hunt.

Exercise brings opportunity. The habits of the Hunt lead to innovations, big and small. Individuals, of course, will have their own habits, some of them quirky, like firing questions at a clerk in the dime store across the street. Indeed, much of what we chronicle throughout this book relates directly to the regular exercise of idea muscles. Setting aside time each day for learning, forging conversations with people outside your normal network of contacts, putting yourself in places where ideas are known to happen (perhaps a book group in which the conversation is rich)—these are all exercise habits.

A fundamental habit of the Hunt is observation—engaging the world around you with eyes wide open, as Sam Walton always did. It's an exercise that requires, among other things, a well-developed sense of what needs to be observed in the first place. It also depends to no small extent on other important habits, such as recording—keeping track of things you've seen and heard. The act of observation is greatly enhanced by another habit: prototyping. By that we mean putting your thoughts and ideas in some tangible form, as a matter of routine. We look at this cluster of habits in the following pages.

Begin with an Eye

Yogi Berra once commented, "You can observe a lot just by watching." The people at IDEO, an exemplar product design firm, have another way of putting it: "Innovation begins with an eye." They're talking about keen observers like Scott Cook, founder of Intuit, who sat at a kitchen table with his wife in 1982 while she paid bills and balanced the checkbook. It was not one of her favorite tasks; she told her husband she could think of few things more tedious and repetitive. And Cook began wondering if there could be a way to

75

"quicken" the process of paying bills. He left his job as a management consultant and launched Intuit with its first product, Quicken, which went on to become the most popular software program for personal finance.

Jim Koch's eye is one of his prized assets. "I don't get ideas sitting in a room thinking," he told us in an interview. "I get them when I'm working the markets."

The Boston Beer Company founder has made a habit of traveling to various cities and spending time in retail stores that sell beer (as many as twenty a day), just looking. During one excursion, in a large liquor store in Denver, he noticed an entire refrigerator case filled with four-packs of higher-strength beer. At that time Koch's company had only sporadically produced that type of beer, which tends to cost more and is therefore more profitable than regular six-packs. Koch recalled that as he stood in front of the cooler, "I thought—wait a minute. We don't have anything in that door. And we should." In a matter of months, Boston Beer was rolling out its four-pack "imperial" series of higher-strength beer. For Koch, getting into this line of beer products turned out to be a "no-brainer," but even such a straightforward idea has to come from somewhere. And it might not have come to Koch, or might not have come quickly enough to gain market share, if he weren't in the habit of looking in stores.

"To me, the ideas come from real-world stimulation," from a conversation, a visit with a wholesaler, and many other contacts, Koch says. On one such occasion, Koch found himself staring at huge stacks of Samuel Adams beer in an independent warehouse. In the beer industry, most wholesalers insist on keeping a month's worth of inventory on hand, to be sure they never run out of beer. But Koch looked at those stacks and said to himself, "Nothing good is happening to my beer as it sits here." It was losing freshness and ultimately adding to costs, because inventory is not free. That observation has prompted Koch to experiment with a new system that aims to slash inventory down to a week or two. It's a replenishment model in which Boston Beer sends wholesalers exactly what they need, when they need it—not necessarily the quantities they want. (The model is made possible by the fact that beer makers can now peer into the computers of wholesalers and see orders from retailers and other relevant data.) Koch's goal is to give people a perfectly fresh beer practically all of the time, which is not a priority for most beer makers.

Just looking can do a lot for someone's business. But having a good eye isn't enough. If it were, then any well-functioning animal would be able to shape an innovation. Presumably, many beer executives have stood in the warehouses and looked at the tall stacks of beer without instituting a whole new inventory system. Observation requires a framework. Part of Koch's framework is his desire to offer the freshest beer in the industry. This is part of his mission, his gig as a high-end beer producer; it's a passion for him. He recalled realizing after visiting several warehouses: "Wow, I can improve the quality of the beer, and I can save everybody money. That, for me, is really exciting." That's the value of observation, fueled by a purpose.

Observing at the Ritz

It's much easier to come up with valuable ideas when the frameworks and structures of observation are in place. Ritz-Carlton, which has created nothing less than a culture of observation, has codified that principle. The culture begins with a strong sense of who each employee is as a member of the organization. For example, Horst Schulze, the charismatic former president of the hotel group, used to say in talks to housekeepers, room servers, and other frontline employees, "You are not servants. We are not servants. Our profession is service. We are Ladies and Gentlemen, just as the guests are, who we respect as Ladies and Gentleman. We are Ladies and Gentleman and should be respected as such."

Hence the official motto of the organization: "Ladies and Gentlemen serving Ladies and Gentlemen." The clear message here is that employees should be respected but also that much is expected of them. The general expectation is that they should be well-exercised for the Hunt. They must be constantly looking for ideas that improve service, which they do principally by way of observation. When it comes to the Ritz, we speak from our own experience as customers.

Part of that experience dates back to a very late night some years ago when we trudged up to the front desk at the Ritz-Carlton in downtown Hong Kong. We were hoping to get to our rooms quickly and grab a few hours of sleep before running a workshop there the next morning. But at the desk we heard the seven words dreaded by every bleary-eyed traveler: "Sorry, there's no reservation in that name." The Ritz had bungled our reservations. Acknowledging the mistake, repentant representatives swiftly booked us into a competitor's hotel down the street, which was, of course, the least they could do.

Making small talk with the desk clerks while the mess was being sorted out, we mentioned our interest in scoring some authentic Chinese food during our brief visit to Hong Kong. One of the clerks asked us to stay put for a moment, disappeared into a back room, and returned with a sheet of scribbled-on notepaper. He told us, "This restaurant is the best in town. Go there tomorrow night, tell them who you are, and I guarantee you'll get a table." When we arrived there the next night, the dining room was packed, but we did indeed get a table, and we had a fabulous dinner. At the end of the meal, we were surprised when the chef came out personally to say that he hoped we enjoyed everything. "And by the way," he added, "this is on the Ritz-Carlton. They want to apologize for inconveniencing you last night."

The Ritz messed up—and made up for it. But our point is not about the kung pao chicken or even the world-class service at the Ritz, for which it is famous. What's more important is the whole apparatus of observation that had to be set in motion to achieve the end result. People at the Ritz had to be paying close attention to us and to what we were saying. They also had to be recording their observations and filtering them through a chain of frontline employees.

The next morning, as we settled in for our executive training session at the Ritz, Andy decided to start sniffing around. He struck up conversations with employees about their ways of detecting things, and they invited him into back rooms where they showed him flip charts (in Chinese and English) revealing a host of service strategies. We learned how Ritz-Carlton employees fill out "Guest Incident Action Forms" that size up mishaps like ours, including registering the guest's reaction to the unfortunate event on a scale from "livid" to "calm." In other words, people at the Ritz were attentive to us and to our states of mind. They were also recording their observations and using them to inform everyone else who had dealings with us during our stay.

Chatting with cleaning people in the hallways, we also learned how they get their ideas about catering to each guest (apart from the lamentable "incidents"). For one thing, Sherlock Holmes's famous rebuke, "You see, Watson, but you do not observe," would not apply. These particular sleuths keep their eyes peeled on guests, constantly picking up clues about their individual likes and dislikes. They take notes and relay word to customer-service people, who, in turn, feed this knowledge into a corporate-wide database. So, if you like working out at the gym, you might find extra towels in your room the next time you check into a Ritz-Carlton hotel, whether you're in Hong Kong or Houston. Bill, for example, is greeted there with extra feather pillows.

Erecting a Personal Platform of Observation

Most people do not work for organizations that provide such an elaborate apparatus of observation. Almost any professional, however, can take steps toward creating similar frameworks and structures that make possible the flow of useful observations. Anyone can begin building a *personal platform of observation.*

To begin with, it helps immensely to know what you're looking for—what deserves keen observation and what doesn't. Ritz-Carlton employees do not observe indiscriminately. They focus on incidents and customer preferences that connect clearly with any hotel services that might enhance their mission as "Ladies and Gentlemen serving Ladies and Gentlemen." For example, a waiter delivering room service will pay less attention to what a guest is watching on television than to the fact that the hotel failed to stock his favorite beverage in the mini-bar.

Nobody can sharply observe *everything* there is to see. In another Sherlock Holmes tale, for example, Dr. Watson was surprised to find that his learned friend did not know the order of the planets and moons in the solar system. Holmes replied: "I consider that a man's brain originally is like a little empty attic, and you have to stock it with such furniture as you choose. A fool takes in all the lumber of every sort that he comes across, so that the knowledge which might be useful to him gets crowded out . . . it is of the highest importance, therefore, not to have useless facts elbowing out the useful ones."

Knowing what to observe closely is a challenge; so is finding ways to bolster the whole endeavor. For one thing, an adequate support system for observation will inevitably involve a time commitment. Learning in general requires time, and the same goes for the part of learning that involves direct observation. It took time for Jim Koch, for example, to travel to other cities and check out stores that sell his Samuel Adams beer. That said, however, much of what needs to be observed can be done as part of normal routine, requiring no extra time at all.

Consider room service at the Ritz. In a documentary program about the hotel chain, a Ritz-Carlton manager in Atlanta explained,

> The waiter has a few moments where . . . the guest . . . is just talking, and the guest may say, "Well, you know, I love your hotel, but I've had a little difficulty getting my favorite beverage." And our room service waiter is kind of prompted to say, "Well, what is that?" And then we find out that information. Room service waiter records it on a slip that is turned in to our Guest History Department. That's put into the computer and it's one more aspect of our customer's history. . . . Next time he comes, we're waiting for him with this particular want or desire.

You can take the lesson of how Ritz employees get ideas in the normal course of work and apply it to your situation. For example, in meetings or even in informal conversations, do you ask questions with the intent of finding new ideas? This does not add to your work time—you're already in the meeting.

Training yourself to notice things is another part of the observational platform. In line with Aristotle's dictum related earlier ("What we have to learn to do, we learn by doing"), the best advice is to be a more deliberate observer, wherever you find yourself.

Paying attention to your own experiences as a customer or client is a good place to start. When you walk into a coffee shop, do the baristas look happy or harried? What can you learn about an establishment from the people who patronize it—how they're dressed or who they're with? Do you have any trouble getting the information you need as a customer?

Making an effort to observe your own customers is even more to the point. Clothing company L.L.Bean has made a habit of sending people out to observe customers who are using the company's products. A team might go to a mountain and watch customers hiking with Bean boots or snowshoes, for instance. "The [L.L.Bean] interviewer's job is to ask open-ended questions in a way that is non-leading and then just to be very quiet and let the customer go," explains David Garvin of the Harvard Business School, who has worked with the company on these projects. From such observations come ideas for new and improved products.

Credit Suisse has a similar practice, in this case sending people into its bank branches to learn about customers. An executive might open a checking account and then watch a customer doing the same. That executive will also talk to the customers, asking how they're experiencing the service. "You can't assume you know what a customer wants until you watch and ask," a Credit Suisse vice president told customer experience expert David McQuillen.

Everyone has a customer, whether that person is someone who buys a product or service, or a fellow employee who is served internally in an organization. You may not have any reason to meet your customers on a mountaintop, but you can always put yourself in their shoes. What do customers care about? What are their frustrations? What can we learn by talking to them, by paying attention to their body language? The value of engaging with customers and clients is that they inhabit a different world; their cares and concerns are not the same as those of the company they patronize. Bank customers, for example, don't usually love banking; they just want to do the chore as easily as possible. Credit Suisse executives have learned that most customers don't care if the company web site offers a highly sophisticated mutual fund calculator. They just want to make simple transactions on a site that's easy to use.

Involving customers in the idea process, or otherwise learning from them, is a rewarding habit. A worthy exercise would be to set a goal of learning three new things about your customers this week. Observing the quality of service you receive at a restaurant, or how welcomed you feel at another place of business, or how a competitor does things—these are other habits. They're ways of sharpening your instincts for learning through direct observation. And they yield bankable ideas.

Write It Down

Ritz-Carlton employees, Credit Suisse executives, and Sam Walton all recorded their observations unfailingly. Writing down your thoughts and observations—and keeping them in a readily accessible place—are necessary habits of the Hunt. That's partly because most of us do not have photographic memories, but also because ideas tend to arrive in bits and pieces that need to be put together over time. And it's easy to forget a fragment that, standing alone, seems unimportant.

You can do more with your notes than just preserve your observations, however. You can begin editing those observations, weeding out the ones that truly seem unimportant and keeping those that are more relevant to your projects and goals. In fact, recording is one of the first tangible steps toward assembling ideas: Perhaps you'll connect something you heard at a PTA meeting to something you learned in a training program at work. Furthermore, over time, your notes create another valuable resource: an archive of your old ideas and impressions.

Thomas Edison was a tireless note taker. He recorded his thoughts in more than 2,500 notebooks, most of which were at least 200 pages long. "Through Edison's use of notebooks," writes his great-grandniece Sarah Miller Caldicott, together with Michael J. Gelb, "the tangible world of experimentation met the intangible world of imagination." Edison made notes freely, often with rough sketches of incipient ideas or just fragments related to an extensive array of technologies. He would capture his thoughts about products he was developing for the telegraph or railway industries and eventually connect these and other observations to form the basic ideas for something new, like the phonograph. Edison wrote down everything he felt was worth jotting down, but he didn't feel pressure to organize the fragments immediately or unite them into an idea right away. He let that process develop naturally over a period of days, months, years.

One day in 1888, the pioneering nature photographer Eadweard Muybridge went to see Edison, bringing along some of his photos depicting animals in motion. At the time, Edison was looking to improve the phonograph, and he made note of the following intention: to experiment on an instrument that "does for the eye what the phonograph does for the ear." Kathleen McAuliffe, writing about this in *Atlantic Monthly* in 1995, explained: "He went on to describe the parallel between the spiral of images that make up what we now call film and the spiral grooves of the phonograph record." A few years later, the first motion-picture camera evolved from these observations.

Keeping a daily notebook is not for everyone, but there are numerous alternatives for tracking your insights and observations. Some people tuck a sheet of notepaper, with their jottings, into a file folder related to an applicable project. Others attach a sticky note to the edge of a computer screen or onto a bulletin board. Still others shoot e-mails to themselves (with clear subject headings) or store thoughts in a BlackBerry or keep a running log of ideas in a word-processing file. Many do all of the above—and more.

Timing is important. It's best to make a note when the observations are fresh—preferably in real time. Otherwise they may fade or evaporate altogether. Another unfortunate possibility is that you might remember the idea with enough clarity, but only after missing a great opportunity to use it.

The U.S. Army uses an observational method with its Center for Army Lessons Learned. The center's observation teams—typically deployed with the first troops in an operation—look for problems and threats as well as opportunities. Just as important, they record what they see on the spot. Analysts at the center's headquarters in Fort Leavenworth, Kansas, then interpret the data in close conversation with teams on the ground. They issue warnings and offer guidance to field units through the center's web site, often within hours, and post new lessons a few days later. Such was the flow of observation during the wars in the former Yugoslavia during the 1990s, when one of the first teams discovered that snow-covered roads were likely to have hidden mines. Speedy recording and sharing of the information was essential. As one military official told Harvard University's David Garvin, "It would be a shame if a soldier in one battalion made the same mistake tomorrow that was made in a different battalion today."

For most people, failing to put a fresh thought on paper probably won't trigger severe consequences. More likely it'll result in passing up a chance to boost efficiency or otherwise enhance the job they're doing. Driving home after a late-day meeting, you might have a rush of ideas about a report you'll be submitting next month. Those thoughts will probably come in handy when you open the file again in a few weeks and start the drafting, but they won't be there if they're not recorded. And you might not be able to recall them in helpful detail at that point, if you've had a million other things to do and remember since then.

Working in an organization that supplies structure for observation and recording obviously makes the process easier. But don't forget that at the root of it all is an individual who is in the habit of noticing things and moving quickly to put those sightings into play.

"The technology serves us well," a Ritz-Carlton manager said, referring to the company's well-organized observation system. "But it is our people who work at listening, so that we can record the customer's every want and need." He added, "We have one guest who appreciates having seven boxes of Kleenex placed about his room. But it is important to keep in mind that it was an attentive person in housekeeping who discovered that we had a guest with severe allergies who needed those tissues."

Get It Moving

There is a point at which observing and noting give way to prototyping—that is, to rough expressions of an idea. When people hear the word "prototype," they may think of a full-scale mockup of a product, program, or design. We look at it differently, as a less formal, everyday activity. When you map out the possible structure of a presentation you'll be making on behalf of your team, you're prototyping. If you do it legibly enough for someone else to look at, then it's simply a more effective prototype, because you're making it easier to elicit comments from others. A prototype doesn't have to look pretty. It just has to get your idea moving a bit beyond the contours of your brain.

Thomas Edison and Henry Ford prototyped all the time—and often in real time. On one occasion, Ford visited Edison at his laboratory in New Jersey and they talked about the problem of developing an electric storage battery for the automobile. Ford later recalled,

> As I began to explain to him what I wanted, I reached for a
> sheet of paper and so did he. In an instant we found ourselves
> talking with drawings instead of words. We both noticed it at
> the same moment and began to laugh. Edison said: "We both
> work the same way."

They sure did. They both understood that prototyping should begin as early as possible in the process, not just when it's time to show clients a few carefully crafted versions of what's being developed. We will have more to say in the next chapter about prototyping in the context of developing particular ideas. What we're underscoring here is the value of early prototyping, which (often in tandem with recording) begins to set your ideas in motion.

Tangibility is the essential quality of any prototype. That's what allows you to start thinking in practical terms about an idea, to start getting a picture of where it might take you. At the same time, because prototypes can be very rough versions of an idea, you can think more freely and seek to innovate more boldly. You can move ahead without the fear of failing that is too often a killer of innovation.

Creating something that another person can evaluate is the other key advantage of tangibility. It's the secret to effective and efficient conversations with people who might be able to help develop your idea, whether they're members of your team or a friend or acquaintance in another line of work. Making the idea more understandable and with as many details as possible allows people to offer feedback that's faster and more precise than they'd normally be able to give in a short conversation.

Making a prototype also helps you begin to get a sense of which ideas may have legs. The ideas aren't sitting there—they're spinning into action, even at a very early stage. You're getting feedback, which should be gratefully received, testing and reshuffling ideas and setting new ones in motion, all as part of a cycle of continuous improvement. Prototyping is one of the regular exercises of the Hunt.

Observe Yourself

In addition to paying attention to the world around them, all Idea Hunters need to observe themselves. Personal experiences—likes and dislikes, to start with—are a potential source of professional ideas. Think of Scott Cook, who came up with the idea for Quicken, the personal-finance software program, after hearing his wife lament the tedious chore of paying bills the old-fashioned way. Recall also (from the Introduction) Puneet Nanda, who developed the FireFly, the toothbrush with flashing lights, after noticing his daughter's delight in her sneakers with flashing lights.

Being sensitive to your own experiences, alert to your desires and frustrations, is a well-established path to innovation. Another case in point: Phil Schiller, the Apple marketing whiz, and the motivations that led to the creation of the iPod. Schiller explains that iPod project members began not with a grand notion or marketing plan, but with a passion for music combined with frustration surrounding the dominant portable music player of the time, the Sony Walkman. "We were so sick of it that we felt compelled to create something," he told a small group that gathered to hear him at Boston College in November 2008.

Sometimes personal experiences are profound. Paul Hogan, chairman of Home Instead Senior Care, based in Omaha, Nebraska, comes from a large extended family—he has eleven aunts and uncles on his mother's side. Hogan was glad for the strength in numbers when it came time to care for his grandmother as she became progressively weaker, finding it hard even to get out of a chair. He says his "Aha!" moment came in 1994 when he wondered what other people do when they don't have ample family resources to help look after a loved one. That's when Hogan and his wife, Lori, founded Home Instead.

"My family had learned that it's one thing to prepare a meal for a person who lives alone, but that it's something else entirely to have someone there to encourage the person to eat that meal. Having someone there to give reminders about taking medications is also helpful," he told Patricia R. Olsen of the *New York Times*. Companionship is important, too, and it is another of the many nonmedical services that Hogan's company now provides to sixty thousand clients worldwide.

At other times, a personal experience might be hardly classifiable as profound, but nonetheless useful. Sir Richard Branson, the colorful founder of Virgin Atlantic Airways, recalls that during a flight he took before starting the company, "I wanted to talk to a pretty girl in the next aisle, but I was stuck in my seat the entire flight." That is why Virgin Atlantic now has stand-up bars in its cabins. Branson added in a 2006 *Fast Company* interview that he went into business originally not to make tons of money "but because the experiences I had personally with businesses were dire and I wanted to create an experience that I and my friends could enjoy." Translating such experiences (whether "dire" or not) into business ideas is a habit every professional can cultivate.

There's another sense in which self-observation is important: when it comes to evaluating your progress as an Idea Hunter. We have devised a self-diagnostic tool for quick and simple use (see the Epilogue). For now, it's worthwhile to take a clear-eyed look at these factors:

1. Your level of curiosity—whether you're interested in both the substance of your work and other people's work.
2. Your breadth—whether you're consulting a wide diversity of sources.
3. Your habits—whether your idea search is steady rather than sporadic.
4. Your positioning—whether you're putting yourself in the line of fire of great ideas and building these ideas as you go along. (Such agility will be the focus of the next chapter.)

It becomes clear that this isn't something done once in a blue moon. It has to be part of your daily exercise routine—nurturing the habits of the Hunt.

IDEAWORK #3

Assembling an Idea Portfolio

For choreographer Twyla Tharp, ideas come in cardboard boxes—plain old file boxes, like the ones that line shelves in lawyers' offices. That's where she stores her inspiration and insights. A 1992 recipient of the John D. and Catherine T. MacArthur Fellowship (known as the "genius grant"), Tharp starts every one of her choreography projects with a box. "I write the project name on the box, and as the piece progresses, I fill it up with every item that went into the making of the dance." She keeps notebooks, news clippings, CDs, videos, books, photographs, art objects, and even toys in these boxes. The materials for *Movin' Out*—a dance musical set to Billy Joel's music and lyrics—filled twelve boxes.

Like Tharp, all of us have places we go to for ideas. It may be the *New York Times* (which Tharp scans each day for articles and photographs) or a source of our own making—perhaps a box or a file folder with ideas for a future project.

The task of an Idea Hunter is to add value to these habits by making them explicit. You're far more likely to produce a regular flow of ideas when you're thinking constantly about where and how to get them. When you do that, you're well on your way to assembling an idea portfolio.

The portfolio should contain your active sources of ideas—the ones you scan regularly. It should also include collections of ideas themselves (kept in boxes, for example), because they are also sources, triggering new thoughts (which should then be added to the collection as well) every time they are reviewed. If you think of these sources and collections as a portfolio, you're less likely to take them for granted. Instead, you'll begin to look at them as assets—they are arguably the most vital assets in today's professional markets—and learn to leverage them.

Start by taking stock of your current sources—web sites, blogs, favorite TV shows, books and other print media, friends, family, colleagues, customers, vendors, direct competitors, museums, and so on. We suggest examining your idea sources through a process we call the "portfolio X-ray." The assessment includes asking yourself questions such as these:

- Where and how am I getting ideas?
- What magazines, journals, and papers do I use regularly?
- What useful books have I read recently?
- What web sites do I visit on a regular basis?
- With whom do I converse in order to find ideas?
- Who challenges my ideas and, by doing so, makes me think more effectively?
- Am I interacting with the same people day after day, or am I making new contacts, finding people outside my usual circle and field of expertise?
- Where, if at all, have I missed opportunities for idea exchanges?

Your answers to these questions will help you pinpoint aspects of your Idea Hunt that could stand improvement. For example, it may turn out that you're drawing on too few sources, which would mean you're not working with enough ideas. Or perhaps you're consulting too many sources and finding too much information that is not especially relevant to your goals as a professional and the specific needs of your projects.

Another possibility is that you're not involved in enough interpersonal conversations, whether face to face or through all the other means (phone, e-mail, GoogleTalk, and so on). As we'll see further in Chapter Six, conversations play a critical role in generating the insights and experiences that bring about real innovations. Or maybe all of your professional conversational time is with people who know the same things you know, which dampens the prospects of coming up with fresh ideas.

We suggest keeping a journal for two weeks. Jot down your idea sources as you consult them during that time, noting which ones you tap most often and which ones spark your curiosity or lead you down other worthwhile trails. Or, if you prefer, simply pull out a sheet of paper now and start brainstorming a list. The point is to see your emerging portfolio in a tangible form. How does it look? What critical sources are absent or underrepresented?

There is no right or wrong answer here. You're creating a picture of the way *you* Hunt. Only you know if this is the portfolio you want and need, and much of that assessment will depend on your gig. In other words, the portfolio has to connect with your self-definition and goals as a professional. It also needs to be keyed to the projects that are commanding your attention.

After you assemble your idea portfolio, you need to explicitly manage and monitor it. Consult your sources regularly and systematically, preferably every day. Then ask yourself more questions:

- Which sources create the greatest value for you?
- Which lead to real progress?
- Do you feel you are making progress every day or only in fits and starts?
- What have you observed about how others manage their idea sources?
- Would any of their practices work for you?
- What are you doing now that you didn't do before? And why?

This process will help you realize that some sources might need to be tapped more often, others less often, and still others dropped altogether. Keeping your portfolio fresh and diverse will best serve your evolving needs and challenges.

Tech Box

Once you're working with a productive array of sources, you have to figure out how to store the better ideas that flow from those sources and to make them accessible. As we've seen, choreographer Tharp prefers to collect them in boxes. "Other people rely on carefully arranged index cards," she writes in *The Creative Habit*. "The more technological among us put it all on a computer. . . . Anything can work, so long as it lets you store and retrieve your ideas—and never lose them."

Tharp's boxes are most certainly a storage mechanism. But they also take on a life of their own as she revisits them, adds to them, extracts new ideas from them. (In one box was a news photograph of an ancient pottery shard depicting a communal migration, which sparked an idea that eventually led to Tharp's hand-holding dance, *Westerly Round*.) Such a collection could be filled with ideas from old projects or from projects that never got off the ground. Or it could contain ideas that are coalescing into a new project. Collections of this kind are a distinct part of an idea portfolio.

IDEO, a leading product design firm, is particularly good at keeping ideas and inspiration accessible, in part because much of the company's stockpile of ideas is embedded in objects that on-site designers can see, touch, and play with. IDEO's designers have compiled a shared trove of more than four hundred gadgets in what they call Tech Box, as the technology manage-ment researcher and former IDEO engineer Andrew Hargadon has chronicled. It's a set of tool cabinets at the firm's headquarters in Palo Alto, California, now viewable to the entire company through its intranet (it takes other forms, such as boxes and shelves, at IDEO offices elsewhere). At various times the eclectic array of stuff has included a toy robot, ski goggles, the bot-tom of a Guinness can, and glow-in-the-dark fabric. All the items represent ideas from past or future projects.

The Tech Box is there for inspiration but also for ex-perimentation and practical use in designing products. The toy robot, for example, might have the right sound for something the designers and engineers are work-ing on, or it might serve as a useful prototype for a new product. Other items might have the right click, fit, shape, or heat response.

You don't have to be a product designer to have a Tech Box. Anyone can collect ideas—and in all sorts of ways. The Tech Box could be a file drawer with a collection of old presentations continually revisited when putting together new ones. It could be the folder icons on the desktop of your PC or a dedicated e-mail box where you send yourself articles, notes, and correspondence. Whatever and wherever it is, it should be visible so that it reminds you that the ideas are there, waiting to be used and developed.

Speaking recently with Ronald L. Sargent, the chairman and CEO of Staples, Andy mentioned how important it was to file away an idea rather than let it evaporate. Sargent replied instantly, "I don't file it. I carry it." At that moment the Staples chief pulled out a thick file folder containing active ideas relating to especially important problems that he's addressing and opportunities he's pursuing. The collection may include, on any given day, a clipping from the *Wall Street Journal*, a note written to himself while on a flight, a copy of a PowerPoint presentation, or other useful material. "I carry it with me. All the time," he said.

That's a Tech Box. What distinguishes it from an ordinary file folder is not the object itself but the way it's used. It needs to be close at hand (in Sargent's case, it's literally in hand) whenever a new idea hits you.

As part of your portfolio, your collection of ideas should be reviewed regularly. Every once in a while, set aside a few hours to revisit all of your idea collections. Read, touch, and ponder. You may discover a new use for an idea or see connections that eluded you before—or you may notice that some of your ideas no longer fit with your gig. Jettison those to open up space for the ideas that you're Hunting for today.

Sargent routinely inspects his folder of especially active ideas. "You look at it and say, 'I thought this was a good idea six months ago, but it's not now. I'm going to throw that one away,'" he told Andy. Just as often, he'll realize that some item recently clipped or copied fits with a problem or project he's been worrying over.

Used in such a fashion, a Tech Box collection keeps delivering ideas you need, when you need them.

I D E

Agile

CHAPTER 5

Idea Flow Is Critical

WEST SIDE STORY IS ONE OF the most enduring classics of American musical theater. It has been revived recently on Broadway and performed over and over again in schools and regional theater companies around the United States. A Shakespearian tragedy made into a popular 1961 motion picture, it is a story of romance, and of rivalry between . . . Catholics and Jews?

If that doesn't sound right, it's because most people know *West Side Story* as a tale of bloodletting between white and Puerto Rican gangs on the Upper West Side of Manhattan. But the original idea was to produce a play called *East Side Story*, with the drama centering on hostilities between Italian Catholics and Jews, culminating in a Passover rumble. It was a bad idea, because the days of Catholic-Jewish rumbling on the streets of New York were numbered by the time the illustrious creative team behind this production first came together in 1949. That team consisted of the composer Leonard Bernstein, the choreographer Jerome Robbins, and the writer Arthur Laurents. They each decided to shelve the idea and went on to pursue separate projects.

Six years later in Hollywood, Bernstein was writing the musical score for *On the Waterfront*, the 1954 film classic starring Marlon

Brando. By the pool at the Beverly Hills Hotel one day, he ran into Laurents. The two were chatting when, at the same time, they both happened to glance at a newspaper someone was holding. The headline was about gang fights between California residents and Mexican immigrants in Los Angeles. As Bernstein recalled later on, "Arthur and I looked at one another . . . [and] suddenly it all sprang to life. We could feel the music and see the movement. It was electric. We could visualize the future product." What they visualized, of course, was the dance of battle between Puerto Ricans, who had recently begun their migration to New York, and white gangs.

Though Bernstein and Laurents had gone their separate ways in 1949, they had kept their problematic idea in motion. And they had kept *themselves* in motion. The composer and the writer stayed on the Idea Hunt even while enjoying a swim, agilely shifting toward another idea source (the newspaper) as they picked up their *East Side Story* conversation. Because the original concept was still alive, it instantly morphed into something fresh when Bernstein and Laurents saw the headline. Upon their return to Manhattan, they put the notion to Robbins, shifted back to team mode, and the *West Side Story* project was reignited.

Here we want to make a point that may sound off-message: the goal of the Hunt is not necessarily to get a great idea, all at once. The objective is to set an idea in motion, letting it stretch, ripen, morph, or otherwise develop in collision and combination with other ideas. That's how an idea becomes great. Whether you have a good idea, a bad idea (like Catholic-Jewish rumbling), or maybe an odd notion that's hard to assess at first, success will depend heavily on whether it's put into a flow of other ideas.

Consider the idea behind the animation blockbuster *Ratatouille*, about a rat who aspires to be a celebrated Parisian chef. On its face, is that a good idea? A bad idea? Hard to say. The well-known company that produced the movie is Pixar, the studio that also created

A Bug's Life, Toy Story, Cars, The Incredibles, and other favorites. The people at Pixar adhere explicitly to the notion that a good idea is not the most important thing when seeking to create a new product. More pivotal, in their view, is a smart and talented team. That's undoubtedly important. But in our opinion, what they are really talking about is something else: idea flow.

Pixar cofounder Ed Catmull points out that the "high concept" (for example, a rodent who dreams of culinary greatness in the human world) is just the first step in a long, plodding process. "A movie contains literally tens of thousands of ideas. They're in the form of every sentence; in the performance of each line; in the design of characters, sets, and backgrounds; in the locations of the camera; in the colors, the lighting, the pacing," he wrote in a September 2008 *Harvard Business Review* article, "How Pixar Fosters Collective Creativity." In this case, Pixar stuck with the high concept of a gourmet rat, which itself must have been the product of many disparate ideas and connections. But the concept was not fleshed out until all those other ideas—having to do with the storyline, characters, and technical features—entered the flow.

A good flow is critical because ideas usually do not start out auspiciously. Seldom are they served on a silver platter, fully baked with all the trimmings. More often than not, they'll appear as a single ingredient, perhaps a barely recognizable one, which needs to be cooked together with many other ingredients. In other words, an idea will often originate as a weak signal—a fragment here, a suggestion there.

Mary Kay Inc., a global direct sales company, began as the faintest of signals. In the early 1950s, Mary Kay Ash was selling mops and other household cleaning products at a house party in Texas, when she noticed something. It was the remarkably smooth complexions of the women there, which they owed to a homemade facial cream offered by their friend, the hostess. At the time, Mary

103

Kay Ash was driven to be the best mop saleswoman she could be, and she could have easily forgotten about the women's complexions (or not even noticed this weak signal in the first place). But she was interested in the skin cream: the hostess sent her home with a bottle, and it gave her face a similar glow.

Over the years she kept going back to the woman's house to refill the bottle, both for her personal use and for her Hunt. She sought out the hostess's father, a tanner who had devised a fluid for softening the hides of livestock. When he realized that the fluid also softened his hands, he concocted the formula for the beauty cream. "Millions of satisfied Mary Kay users around the world today can thank some scarred horse's ass for their radiant complexions," the economist Todd G. Buchholz remarked in his book *New Ideas from Dead CEOs.*

But Mary Kay Ash was barely in mid-flow of ideas tracing back to the house party. After buying the rights to the tanner's formula in 1963, she opened a retail skin-care and cosmetics outlet in Dallas—which failed. She started keeping a notebook of both good and bad ideas she had picked up while working for various direct-sales companies. She struck up conversations with colleagues and others about how to motivate a sales force. There were other ideas to be found, tested, and tried. Along the way there were also personal trials—the loss of a job, the death of her first husband. But the ideas stayed in motion, leading to what would become a global independent network of more than two million sales people.

The Case of the Guitar Strings

How do you keep ideas in flow? One way is by keeping yourself in the flow—putting yourself in the line of fire of potentially valuable ideas. Much of this has to do with lessons highlighted in previous chapters, about getting into the habit of looking for ideas every-where, all the time. What we want to pinpoint here is the act of moving toward different sources of ideas and consciously beginning to work with those ideas. This requires agility—the kind that Mary Kay Ash showed when she was selling cleaning products at the house party and suddenly fixed her attention on the women using the facial cream. Putting herself in motion, she also gravitated to other idea spaces, including the place (wherever it was) that she met up with the tanner. We picture her in a barn, staring down at a horse's rump, in search of ideas about women's skin care.

How W. L. Gore came to produce top-selling guitar strings is a story of idea flow. In theory, Gore had no business getting into a market populated by such grand names of the guitar world as Mar-tin, Gibson, and Guild. Gore was known primarily for its popular fabric GORE-TEX, although it uses the basic technology for a range of applications including medical devices. Back in the 1990s, one of its engineers, Dave Myers, was working on a project to develop ar-tificial arteries. Like some of his colleagues at the Gore plant in Flagstaff, Arizona, Myers was also an avid mountain biker. So, while working on a coating for the artificial arteries, he also started ex-perimenting with gear cables, using the same material. He wanted to produce cables that would allow the gears on his bike to shift more smoothly.

That he did. Gore added mountain-bike cables to its lines of products and extended the application to the cables used to animate puppets at Disney World and Chuck E. Cheese's. For his work on the cables, Myers had used guitar strings as his principal prototype. Job done, he might have had every reason to toss the strings—coated with polytetrafluoroethylene, or PTFE, the original Gore fabric material—into the waste basket. Instead, he kept them in the flow.

Not a musician himself, Myers asked a few amateur guitarists what they thought of the coated strings. He had a notion that the strings would feel smoother to the touch, but what really impressed the guitar players, after weeks of picking and strumming, was that the strings kept their tone longer than conventional strings. In 1995, after much more experimenting and prototyping, Gore unveiled Elixir Strings, which last three to five times longer than conventional strings. For guitarists, as well as mandolin and banjo players, this means they don't have to restring so often—which is nobody's favorite chore. That's why Elixir, which also costs more than other brands, is now perched on top of the market.

Myers demonstrated great agility. He started with ideas for his work on artificial arteries (which, by the way, became another successful Gore product). Those ideas stayed with him as he pedaled into other idea spaces, including the mountain-biking scene of northern Arizona, which ostensibly had nothing to do with his job. Out of that flowed the ideas for bike gears and puppet cables. Then he stepped into an idea space he was completely unfamiliar with— guitar playing. The guitar strings that Myers used as gear-cable prototypes were essentially a weak signal, a faint glimmer of another idea. He followed the signal, and the result was the first major innovation in guitar-string technology in more than two decades.

If Myers and others at Gore hadn't kept pedaling, not one of those products would have seen the light of day.

Creating Idea Spaces at Pixar

Dave Myers was able to keep himself in the line of fire of ideas, and he used those ideas as they sprang forth from dissimilar idea spaces. One company that thinks out loud about how to create the conditions for such idea flow is Pixar. It wants to make sure its employees are getting ideas from all directions, both inside and outside the organization.

The very design of Pixar's main building in Emeryville, California, exemplifies the plan. The structure was the brainchild of Apple CEO Steve Jobs, who cofounded Pixar in 1986 (he sold it to Disney two decades later). Jobs wanted to ratchet up the odds of people interacting with each other, so he built a large atrium in the middle of the building. (Rumor has it that his original design called for just one bathroom in the entire building, in the interest of facilitating further idea-exchange, but Pixar staff rebelled against this particular innovation.)

When the building opened in 2000, some saw the atrium as a waste of space. But Brad Bird, who directed *Ratatouille* and *The Incredibles*, among other Pixar films, explained in a *McKinsey Quarterly* interview in 2008:

> The reason [Steve Jobs] did it was that everybody goes off and works in their individual areas. People who work on software code are here, people who animate are there, and people who do designs are over there. Steve put the mailboxes, the meetings rooms, the cafeteria, and, most insidiously and brilliantly, the bathrooms in the center—which initially drove us crazy—so that you run into everybody during the course of a day. He realized that when people run into each other, when they make eye contact, things happen. So he made it impossible for you not to run into the rest of the company.

Space matters. Studies of organizational space have shown that just a few meters can make a difference in the number of cross-fertilizing conversations that take place. Put a little too much distance between the animation room and the music department, and there will be fewer such encounters. The Pixar building was designed to increase the likelihood of conversations, to maximize the chances of encountering an idea. Most people don't work in such surroundings, but everyone can be more idea-savvy about the spaces they occupy during the course of a day. To begin with, you could identify the places where ideas are most likely to be flowing. You could also act with the understanding that an office or a meeting room is not the only place to field an idea—sometimes it's not even the best place. The cafeteria might often be a better bet, especially when the purpose is to nibble on ideas.

Jorma Ollila, current chairman and former CEO of Nokia, used to visit Silicon Valley for up to three months a year, just to be part of the region's idea scene. He once told Bill that during his most productive visits to companies in the Valley, he often never made it beyond the cafeteria. The conversations sprang up naturally in that setting and the ideas started flying. Such a borderless environment allowed for more people to join in the conversation, more brains to be tapped, and more ideas to be put into flow. It's not surprising that later on, when Nokia built its new headquarters in Finland, one of the building's two atriums was used solely as the cafeteria. Many of the offices had glass walls with a full view of the cafeteria. The message was clear: Come down and join the conversation.

At Pixar, physical space is only part of what puts people in the stream of ideas. The company's Pixar University, for example, offers in-house courses in such business-related subjects as screenplay writing and drawing (as well as non-business-related pursuits like yoga), and is intended to bring employees together across specialties and disciplines. That is one way to multiply the idea spaces people inhabit.

Another way is to extend those spaces beyond the organization. Pixar encourages its technicians to share their ideas with others in the computer animation industry as well as with people in the academic community. They do so primarily by publishing their ideas in professional journals and presenting them at conferences. "Publishing may give away ideas, but it keeps us connected with the academic community," Catmull wrote in the *Harvard Business Review*. He says the openness helps reinforce the belief throughout the company that "people are more important than ideas."

Let's say it another way: putting people in motion with ideas is often more important than the ideas themselves, which are all subject to idea flow.

Essentially, Pixar's employees keep one foot in the organization and another in different external professional communities. The company wants its people to span boundaries—for the purposes of organizational idea flow. Leonard Bernstein was a so-called "boundary-spanner." He used to explain his behavior this way: "When I'm with composers, I say I'm a conductor. When I'm with conductors, I say I'm a composer." Think about how such agility helps move ideas from one community to another.

Still another way that Pixar enlarges its thinking space is to welcome ideas from misfits and malcontents. They're the people who are on their way out the door because their weird, wild, or just plain different ideas aren't being given an opportunity to grow. "So I said, 'Give us the black sheep.' I want artists who are frustrated. I want the ones who have another way of doing things that nobody's listening to," recalls Brad Bird. He was referring specifically to how he recruited staff for *The Incredibles*, a project that some said could not be done because it required new and costly technologies. "We gave the black sheep a chance to prove their theories, and changed the way a number of things are done here. For less money per minute than was spent on the previous film, *Finding Nemo*, we did a movie that had three times the number of sets and had everything that was hard to do. All this because the heads of Pixar gave us leave to try crazy ideas."

What Pixar demonstrates is that the stream of ideas does not flow in a straight line. It bends and swerves—at one turn, toward people on your team, at another, toward others outside the organization. Pixar also recognizes the value of seeking out those who inhabit marginal idea spaces (the black sheep), and in doing so the company follows the advice of Tom Peters, who talks up the notion of taking a "weirdo" to lunch. He advises, in *The Brand You 50*, "Purposefully hang out with freaks. (Cool people I can learn cool stuff from)."

In other words, get to the people who hang out in places where you don't normally hang out. It's like making a point of sitting at the geek table in the cafeteria (if you're not a geek). Of course, agility also requires veering toward someone who is at the nexus of knowledge within an organization. As we'll explain in the next chapter, a conversation with one of these knowledge connectors can be a shortcut to valuable ideas, information, and perspectives.

Finding the "Informal Bosses"

Think about the type of projects that most organizations undertake. From whom do the people working on those projects get their ideas? Often it's from other people working on the same projects. Of course, they're an essential source of expertise, information, and know-how. But there are other idea spaces that need to be explored, other people who should be heard from.

In recent years researchers have mined the value of stepping into less-familiar idea spaces. Particularly instructive are some of the studies by sociologist Ronald S. Burt. He has consistently found that standout ideas come from managers who forge conversations with people outside their immediate circles. Those people span what Burt refers to as "structural holes," gaps between different groups of people. A common example of a structural hole in organizational life would be the gaps between sales and engineering staffs. In their day-to-day work, they naturally interact with colleagues in their own spaces or specialties. But they generally don't check out each other's spaces. Engineers, for instance, don't tend to talk to people in sales about what customers are asking for (or not asking for).

Those who stand near the structural holes are "at higher risk of having good ideas," as Burt puts it. And because they have connections across fields and disciplines, they also have "early access to diverse, often contradictory information and interpretations, which gives them a competitive advantage in seeing and developing good ideas. People connected to groups beyond their own can expect to find themselves delivering valuable ideas, seeming to be gifted with creativity." He adds, "This is not creativity born of genius. It is creativity as an import-export business."

In one study conducted in 2000, Burt worked with several hundred supply-chain managers at Raytheon, one of the top military contractors in the United States. He had them jot down ideas for improving the company's supply chain—ideas that were later evaluated by senior executives with long experience in that arena (and who worked in other parts of the country). The managers were also asked if they had talked about the ideas with others in the company, and with whom they had had the most detailed conversations. In the end, the most highly rated ideas came from managers who ventured into less-traveled spaces, sharing their ideas with people beyond their immediate circle.

Most managers were in a position to discuss their ideas across business units if they so chose, but Burt found that "the people with whom they discussed their ideas were overwhelmingly colleagues already close in their informal discussion network." This spelled trouble, because their usual conversation partners tended to look at problems the same way they did and didn't broach alternatives. As a result, their ideas for improvements in supply-chain management were not developed.

What they should have done, according to Burt, was to talk to people outside their usual circle of contacts. He recommended an "informal boss," someone with distance from the operation who is not a higher-up but has influence nonetheless. More broadly, an informal boss is almost anyone in the organization (but outside the group) who can help guide you toward a well-developed idea.

These Raytheon managers found their way to places other managers didn't go, where they could pick up ideas that others were missing. They stood near the holes, the gaps, and the empty spaces between one project, function, or specialty and another. And they did so simply by talking to people (especially the "informal bosses") outside their immediate work groups.

That's not a bad place to start, but there are many other ways of minding the knowledge gaps and exploring the idea terrain. Attending a conference outside your specialty can be very worthwhile, if you're looking for something more than the usual ideas. If you're at a conference in your own field, why not broaden the spaces beyond the formal talks and workshops? The hotel lobby, where some of the conference-goers are playing hooky, or the coffee shop where others are making conversation, might be even better spaces for your Idea Hunt.

Recall the conversation that rebooted the *West Side Story* project, the chance encounter between Leonard Bernstein and Arthur Laurents in Beverly Hills. These two New Yorkers didn't fly to the West Coast to take a swim. Bernstein was there to draft a musical score, and Laurents was pounding out a screenplay (separate projects unrelated to *West Side Story*). But they found their most lasting idea at the hotel swimming pool—outside of the studios and meeting rooms.

Letting Ideas Percolate

Those who get ideas have to start putting them into play—working with them. This means tending carefully to the ideas, teasing out the ones with promise, ushering them toward other ideas and information that might help bring about a useful product. One of our favorite columnists is the *New York Times* science reporter Olivia Judson, who writes about the influence of science and biology on modern life, so we were delighted to read a column she wrote just before leaving for sabbatical in which she revealed some of her idea-flow secrets.

To start with, Judson says it's important to catch ideas as they appear. In her case, she's trying to flag down story ideas, which could come to her at any time—while in the bath, talking to friends, or even falling asleep. She keeps what she calls a "list," but which is really a mess of Post-it notes and scraps that litter her desk. On those scraps are notes like these:

- Seven amusing things to do with bacteria?
- Funny methods? Find paper where scientist dressed as a mouse. . . .
- Do sexually transmitted diseases increase sex drive?
- Oxytocin and diplomacy
- Painting the planet
- Taking names

Obviously those scrawls mean something to Judson they might not mean to others. For example, as she explained, "taking names" alludes to research looking into whether the names people are given at birth affect their lives later on, perhaps because of how they influence the way the world looks at them. Our point is that ideas and impressions need to be recorded somehow. This is a simple way of getting an idea in motion, but it's an early step in the march toward a successful idea.

"Some ideas look great from the bathtub, but turn out to be as flimsy as soup bubbles—they pop when you touch them," she observes. Others are so big and unwieldy that they're hard to handle within the confines of a relatively short newspaper article, and still others, she adds, are a perfect fit. But she doesn't know until she investigates the ideas. She'll look through her favorite science databases, do lots of other reading, talk to colleagues, and follow threads of information to their original sources.

Judson continues: "Having done this, I let the information percolate. Often it takes me several runs at a subject to create something coherent." She referred to a piece she had done a few weeks earlier—about cuckoos—which she had drafted three times previously. The final version was a fusion of a few different subjects she had been investigating. "Perhaps I'll give the full treatment to one of the related subjects when I come back," she wrote.

We'll look forward to reading more when Olivia Judson returns from her sabbatical. For now, let's summarize the soup-to-nuts flow of Judson's ideas. Prior to getting the initial idea in the bathtub, she's casting about, combing through press releases, checking science websites, talking to people who regularly alert her to interesting papers. And she's ready to receive the ideas wherever she might be and from whomever she might be with. She jots those ideas down. Judson moves the ideas further by getting more ideas—from databases, for example. She gives herself time to absorb the whole spread of notions, and then she moves into full-scale prototyping. She'll write a few columns on the same subject, before settling on one version or combining them into a final product.

Prototyping is a tool that works in virtually all phases of the Idea Hunt. Judson was starting to prototype when she initially put her thoughts on sheets of paper, which allowed her a first glimpse of her notion in tangible form. She continued prototyping by talking to people about the story idea, which is a way of testing the concept. And she wrote versions of a single column knowing full well that only one would survive in the end as a published product; the other versions would remain on the cutting-room floor. That was a way of building failure into the process—another function of prototyping. As they say at the design firm IDEO: fail often, to succeed sooner.

Writing is, of course, a solitary craft. Prototyping offers further advantages to people working on teams and in other intensely collaborative environments. At Pixar, animators constantly show their work in an early, incomplete form to the entire animation crew. This makes communication among team members easier and faster, accelerating the flow of ideas and improving the likelihood of solid feedback. In addition, with such an approach "people learn from each other and inspire each other; a highly creative piece of animation will spark others to raise their game," Ed Catmull points out. Yet another advantage is that there are normally fewer surprises at the end of a prototyping process. "When you're done, you're done," says Catmull. "People's overwhelming desire to make sure their work is 'good' before they show it to others increases the possibility that their finished version won't be what the director wants." Or what the director of marketing wants.

With prototyping, the Idea Hunt reaches a new level. You're not just putting yourself in the flow of ideas. You're creating a flow, moving ahead with something tangible, something you and others can picture and turn into an item of conversation, of action. That's how an idea grows.

When It's Time to "Kill" Ideas

The ideas can pile up in such a robust flow. And this raises a question of quantity. How do you handle what will—or should—become an oversized load of ideas? We say "should" because of a general rule we apply: the more ideas the better, in the early stages of a project or innovation. Remember Catmull's point about how a movie contains "literally tens of thousands of ideas." You could probably say something similar about the design of a shopping cart—which the people at IDEO know something about. Company founder David Kelley makes a reasonable case for quantity. "If you're forced to come up with ten things, it's the clichéd things that you have off the top of your head," he says. "But if you have to come up with a hundred, it forces you to go beyond [the clichés]."

That's true enough, in our experience. But then how do you start winnowing down and selecting the best ideas? Part of the answer gets back to a kind of prototyping. If it's important to put a single idea down on paper or in some other form, as we've seen, it's just as important get a handle on all the ideas collected in the flow. For example, if you're preparing a sales presentation, you'll want to somehow make visible the ideas you have for making that pitch. For such a task, often one sheet of paper and a pencil will do.

There are other ways of capturing the entire idea flow, which is the first step toward picking and choosing well. Walt Disney and his team liked to use storyboards, which started out as sheets of paper with rough sketches of movie scenes, pinned up on bulletin boards. He used a storyboard when rounding up ideas about what people might want to see in a theme park—what kinds of rides, whether there should be trains, and so forth. Speaking of the method and his boss, project member and Disney art director Richard Irvine once recalled, "We would just . . . put up our ideas, write our ideas on squares of paper, put them on a board, and he'd come down in the afternoon and sit there and look at them and juggle them around. . . . And eventually it evolved"—into Disneyland.

But how does the final rendering of ideas, what we would call a final prototype, evolve? Individuals and teams have their own approaches, geared to different kinds of work and projects as well as learning behaviors. We like the way L.L.Bean goes about whittling down ideas from customers. In the last chapter, we mentioned that the company sends teams out to customers' homes and hunting lodges and other settings, to talk with people about Bean products they use. Let's pick up the story from there, with research conducted by Harvard University's David Garvin, who produced an illuminating video presentation of Bean's idea process.

The case in point is a project to develop a new hunting boot. The product development team spends much time interviewing game hunters and writing everything down—comments like, "I wrecked a pair of the L.L.Bean Maine Hunting Boots the first couple of years I was bird hunting because the briars and the general friction created in the cover used to pick at the stitching from the leather top to the rubber bottom. . . ." After each interview, team members interpret what the customer said. They do so primarily by organizing the comments into what the company calls "voices and images," which Garvin translates as "evocative quotes" and "vivid descriptions." Presumably a quote might be "I wrecked a pair" of boots and a description might be of the hunter running his finger along the stitching that came undone.

There will be hundreds of voices and images, quotes and descriptions. The team has to not only digest them but also translate them into a set of requirements for the refashioned boot. At this point the product development teams goes into seclusion for three days. They employ a version of the Disney storyboards, splattering a wall with sticky notes—hundreds of them—each one articulating a product requirement. (We'll take a wild guess and say one of the requirements was to do something about the leather stitching.) Then they begin trimming down the list of requirements. One way is simply by voting. Why not? It's a team, and the members need to begin working collaboratively with a leaner list of ideas. There are several rounds of voting.

From there, they organize the requirements into clusters, each with a single statement. At the end of the three-day ritual they have a poster displaying a final list of requirements, roughly a dozen altogether. "It's a shared interpretation of the customer's world that will guide the team's design of the new hunting boot," Garvin observes. A brainstorming session a few weeks later helps to further develop and refine the required features of the boot. At that stage, L.L.Bean is three months away from a full-scale mockup of its new product.

Undoubtedly this is an excellent way to produce a hunting boot. But does the process have any bearing on how to develop ideas for other products, services, and systems, or routine tasks like putting together a presentation? We think it does. The general takeaway is that (1) there's value in tabulating all the ideas, in a form that's viewable; and (2) there are ways of getting the ideas down to a manageable few. (These tasks are another aspect of agility in the handling of ideas.) Furthermore, it's worth having an established method—or, preferably, a batch of methods—for paring down the ideas. Most of us have techniques of one kind or another, whether or not we're fully conscious of them. Giving the matter some thought makes it more likely that we'll improve upon those methods.

Specifically, the voice-and-image technique might apply to a range of situations. For example, any Idea Hunt will involve getting and using feedback, whether from customers, people inside the organization, or others. The feedback could be captured in a list that includes the most valuable comments (voices or quotes) and your own thoughts provoked by the comments. The next steps could involve assessing and ranking the feedback, followed by connecting to your plans everything you've heard. Gradually the cacophony of voices gives way to your own voice, your own thoughts about how to use the feedback and go forward. Whatever the approach, the key is to make the ideas visible, and to start making decisions about them.

Some of those decisions will be tough. Robert Sutton, a professor of management science and engineering at Stanford University, tells of a visit that Steve Jobs paid to Yahoo! headquarters in Sunnyvale, California. Jobs was invited to speak with the company's top brass (one of whom funneled this account to Sutton). During the meeting, they came around to the subject of bad ideas and the task of purging them. That's no sweat, Jobs told the Yahoo! leaders. Almost anyone can do that. The hard part, he stressed, is killing off good ideas—which must be done.

His point was that any successful idea requires a vast amount of attention (read: resources), and there are only so many ideas that can get this sort of treatment. Many good ones will have to go. "The challenge is to be tough enough to do the pruning so that the survivors have a chance of being implemented properly and reaching their full potential," Sutton wrote in a blog post titled "If You're the Boss, Start Killing More Good Ideas."

We would quibble with the word "killing." It sounds so final. As we've said elsewhere, old ideas can be valuable resources for an Idea Hunter. They need to be stored somewhere, perhaps literally on a shelf, as some of the most innovative companies make a point of doing. More often than not, the deferred ideas will live to fight another day, return to flow another time. But Jobs and Sutton are onto something. At some point, good ideas need to start exiting the innovation process, or they'll start mucking it up. Worse yet, they'll end up in a final product that's ill-defined and tries to do too much.

We started this chapter with what might have sounded like an off-message—that the goal of the Hunt is not to get good ideas right away but to set all of the ideas in motion. And now, we end by striking another dissonant chord: start ejecting some of your good ideas.

Ready, Set, Launch

At the end of a trail of ideas, you will have—with any luck—an excellent idea with the potential to make a difference. Even a first-rate idea, however, will not sell itself. You have to make sure your idea gets the attention it deserves and wins the acceptance of bosses, clients, and others. In short, the idea needs to be launched.

Recall W. L. Gore's fabulous idea—to produce guitar strings that keep their tone longer than all the other guitar strings. The company achieved its goal, but fully developing that idea and selling it in the marketplace turned out to be two different propositions. One problem was with W. L. Gore itself: the company was known for its breathable GORE-TEX fabric but not for anything having to do with musical instruments. Another obstacle was the new product's price—initially three times that of regular strings.

W. L. Gore used a few major strategies to draw attention to its product, Elixir Strings. Most effective was its decision to seek out an alliance with a stellar name in the guitar world—Taylor Guitars. The guitar manufacturer agreed to put Elixir Strings on every guitar shipped out to retail stores, together with a tag explaining how a special coating made Elixir last several times longer than conventional strings. Taylor's name caught the attention of retailers, which had been skeptical of Elixir's hefty price, and led in turn to acceptance by guitar players. Elixir is now the leading brand of strings for fretted instruments.

Good brand association—connecting your product to a known quantity, particularly one held in high esteem—was a winning strategy for W. L. Gore. For individual professionals, a good association may be with a person rather than a brand. Identify the people in your organization who have a proven record of success in moving ideas to market, and link your proposal to them in one way or another. Or perhaps, in another time-honored approach, unite your idea with the mission and cherished values of your organization.

Brand association is one of many tactics that can help launch an idea successfully. What follows are several guidelines that we have found especially effective in our work with both individual managers and organizations.

"Gig-Friendliness"

This is a prerequisite of launching an idea. A recurring theme in this book has been the value of discerning what you're all about and where you want to be going as a professional—your gig. Before even trying to associate your idea with a well-regarded team at work, give some final thought to whether you want the idea associated with a particularly significant person: you. The moment of launching may be the final chance to consider some important questions before reaching the point of no return. The key is to determine whether the idea is gig-friendly.

Ask yourself the following:

- Do I enjoy spending time and energy on this initiative?
- Deep down, do I really want to be involved in this project?

- Will I learn something through the launching effort, something that expands my circle of competence, what I'm very good at?
- Do I want to be known as the person who brought this idea to life?
- Can I imagine a set of circumstances in which I would not want to be associated with this idea?

If the answer to any of the first four questions is "no," or the answer to the fifth question is "yes," it might be prudent to shelve the idea or hand it off to someone else and cut your losses.

One Revolution at a Time

You might have the greatest new idea of all time, but it still has to be implemented in the existing world. Someone will say, "Yeah, but how does it fit with the way we do business around here?" It's a fair question. An idea that requires too much change in an organization may not gain acceptance. It's hard to sell more than one revolution at a time.

Let's say you're meeting with colleagues or higher-ups. You're proposing an idea about how to archive and then access customer insights in the company's database, and they're paying attention. Then you mention that they'll have to give up Windows as an operating system. The room falls silent. Suddenly you're talking about a more involved undertaking, and people are perhaps feeling a bit overwhelmed by the implications of all this. Is getting rid of Windows essential to your idea? If it is, you better have a superb argument and plan for converting—with minimal effort and disruption—to a new system.

You don't have to compromise unduly with the forces of inertia. Just try to structure your idea so that it requires no more change than is absolutely necessary. Your idea has to be compatible, or potentially compatible, with the world as you find it. In 1879, Thomas Edison's incandescent light bulb was a revolutionary idea, but a system for distributing electrical power had not yet been created. Edison did not try to invent such an infrastructure. Instead, he found compatibility with the existing system of gas lighting, running electricity through the pipes, fixtures, and meters already in customer homes. He chose to effect just one revolution at a time.

Pressing the Hot Buttons

What keeps senior managers up at night? What are the problems and opportunities that haunt them during the day? What are their fondest dreams and worst nightmares? If you can tie your idea to any of these hot buttons, you'll have a much better chance of winning acceptance.

The hot-button principle was at work in the launching of Elixir Strings. One problem for guitar-store owners was that they had to continually restring their showroom instruments as potential buyers tried out the guitars and wore out the strings. The only alternative, if they didn't want to go through the trouble and expense of putting on new ones, was to let the strings lose their bright tone. The long-lasting Elixir Strings changed all that.

Shop owners could restring their guitars less often without compromising the bright tone that customers liked. That was a huge advantage (which also resolved the issue of the price point, because fewer sets of strings had to be purchased). Today Elixir is installed in the factories of nearly every leading guitar maker that does not manufacture its own strings.

Improvability

Sociologist Randall Collins has researched ways of capturing what he calls a share of "attention space." One strategy is to frame your idea as extending and improving an existing idea. In other words, identify an idea that someone else is working on, agree with it, and add something that expands and improves it.

That was the approach Steve Jobs took in January 2010, when he introduced the iPad, Apple's foray into e-books. "Amazon has done a great job" with the Kindle, Jobs declared at a news conference. "We're going to stand on their shoulders and go a little bit further." This is the principle of improvability, which holds that a product can always be better or adapted for additional uses. The pitch is altogether different from another strategy for gaining attention space— taking a contradictory position, in which you try to demonstrate that a particular idea is completely new, a break with the past.

"Try-ability"

Whenever possible, let people try your idea before they buy into it. As the late communication scholar Ev Rogers demonstrated in his widely influential research, customers and colleagues are far more likely to sign on if they're less worried about making a decision they'll come to regret. That's why America Online gave away millions of system discs. The company believed that recipients were more likely to try AOL if they didn't have to pay for it first. It's also why Apple iTunes is set up so that people can listen to thirty-second snippets of music before they buy a CD. The tracks are try-able.

The principle could apply to almost any idea ready for launch. Someone working in a sales department might have a new format for sales reporting that she would like to promote, for example. Instead of simply arguing for the approach, she could start circulating brief versions of reports in the new format, letting people try it out. They might like it and ask for more.

Focusing on the Benefits

At all times, you need to keep the message simple. This can be challenging for people who are close to an idea and deeply knowledgeable of its ins and outs. Often they'll complicate their message unnecessarily by spending most of the time describing how the idea works. It's much better to instead focus on what stakeholders will get from the idea.

Apple's experience with the iPad is once again illustrative. Undoubtedly the device has many fascinating technical components, but at the news conference Jobs did not spend much time on them. Instead, he enumerated the benefits of the device: browsing the Web, sending e-mail, sharing photographs, watching videos, enjoying music, playing games, and reading e-books. He focused on the users' experience, what they would get from the idea. That's what any target audience will want to know.

Notice what happens once you've settled upon an idea: you need more ideas to launch it. When W. L. Gore couldn't get guitar sellers to take an interest in its revolutionary brand of guitar strings, it needed ideas—for example, about good brand association. When Steve Jobs planned his pitch to the public for the iPad, he needed ideas—about extending Amazon's work with Kindle.

You don't stop thinking and searching once you have a fully developed idea. The Hunt continues.

CHAPTER 6

Create Great Conversations

ON A JULY EVENING IN 1937, the renowned conductor Leopold Stokowski was alone having dinner in a Los Angeles restaurant when he saw someone at another table trying to get his attention. "Why don't we sit together?" the other patron called over. That man was Walt Disney, who had just acquired the rights to *The Sorcerer's Apprentice*, a symphonic piece based on a poem by Goethe. Disney immediately asked Stokowski what he thought of the musical score and mentioned that he was thinking of turning it into a short film, with Mickey Mouse in the lead role.

There was further talk of collaboration between the two giants, who each represented a different genre of entertainment. Afterward, Disney wrote to a colleague: "I am greatly enthused over the idea and believe that the union of Stokowski and his music, together with the best of our medium, would be the means of a great success and should lead to a new style of motion picture presentation." The two men began working together, and the project evolved into the motion-picture classic *Fantasia* (released in 1940), which featured the *Sorcerer's Apprentice* in one of its segments. The great conductor himself appeared on screen, at one point shaking hands with Mickey Mouse.

129

To truly appreciate this encounter, one must realize that Disney had other things on his mind that summer. As Michael Barrier relates in his biography *The Animated Man*, Disney and his team were plowing ahead with *Pinocchio*, tangling with some basic questions of animation, like how to draw the main characters. Dining alone at his table and running through the *Pinocchio* sequences in his head, Disney could easily have averted his eyes and avoided Stokowski. He could have said to himself: *Well, if I talk to anyone now, it's going to be someone who knows a lot about animation.* But that wasn't his way.

Disney was a conversationalist, and he used his conversations to get ideas moving. He also wanted to keep stretching his notions of how to be Walt Disney, the impresario of family entertainment. That summer he was immersed in one project and contemplating another that would expand the Disney brand by merging his medium with classical music. He was beginning to dress for his next gig.

It would be hard to identify even one great Idea Hunter who was not in the habit of cultivating great conversations. There are chance conversations, like the kind that helped lead eventually to *Fantasia*, and there are ongoing conversations of the sort you might have with an old friend who is a history buff. There are big conversations, small conversations, conversations with acquaintances, with perfect strangers, with people down the hall, with customers, and with clients. There are conversations with people in the know and conversations with people on the outs—like Pixar's "black sheep" described in the previous chapter.

As we saw in that chapter, putting yourself in the line of fire of ideas is a pivotal step in the innovation process. Conversations are a primary means of stepping into that line, exposing yourself to the onslaught of ideas.

Almost anyone can be a valuable conversation partner, but some people have a unique place in the communication flow. Because of what they know and how they learn, they seem to embody all the essential links in the conversational chain, and they spread their knowledge by way of informal communication. Massachusetts Institute of Technology professor Thomas J. Allen has described these people as "gatekeepers," but perhaps a more apt designation would be "connectors." In Allen's influential research, they are the "switches" through which ideas flow in an organization. They are not normally in the upper echelons of an organization, but they are involved in more conversations than most professionals. Here are some other characteristics of connectors that we have identified:

- They are far more likely than others to keep up with the literature in their field, especially the material that is highly complex and difficult.
- They attend more professional meetings and meet more people there than their colleagues. They also spend more time in bars and at the pool than in the sessions, but they wind up knowing more about the research than those who sat through them.
- They are accessible to unusually large numbers of people.
- They tend to recognize connections between what some people know and what others are looking for, and they make those connections for you.
- They are trusted. You can go to them and admit you don't know what's going on—and your secret is safe. Even better, they'll help you find out what you need to know.

Not everyone can become a connector (and some might not particularly care to). For one thing, according to the research, connectors tend to go unrecognized—and therefore unappreciated—by top management. Allen found that they make up no more than one-tenth of an organization's technical employees (who were Allen's primary subjects). Our point is that, if you're an Idea Hunter, you should figure out who these people are and start building conversations with them.

Buddy DeFranco, one of the greatest jazz clarinetists of all time, was a standout member of almost every great swing band of the mid-twentieth century. He used to hang around with jazz pianist Michael "Dodo" Marmarosa, who played for the bandleader Artie Shaw. "Dodo was always rather eccentric. But he had a great, not only technical ability, but . . . a great ability to hear new things," DeFranco recalled years later. "He had a concept for grasping new ideas—playing new ideas. Dodo was always searching, always into new things. . . . a lot of new things escaped me. But I was smart enough to hang onto Dodo. Because he knew. He knew. And I knew he knew."

DeFranco certainly qualified as an Idea Hunter. He realized that his career depended on the acquisition of new ideas, and he was humble enough to know that he needed help in identifying those ideas. He figured that he could position himself in the middle of an idea flow by glomming onto Dodo and creating great conversations with him.

Dodo was a connector. Who is connecting you to the ideas that will help fill gaps in your Hunt, help keep you in a continued flow of fresh ideas? Who's your Dodo?

"Continuers" and "Terminators"

Conversations are building blocks of innovation, ways to move an idea from origination to application. But they often stall at the starting gate or become unproductive. To create successful conversation, make sure you're sending the right signals to your conversation partners, letting them know you're interested in a real exchange of ideas. Recent studies of how doctors talk to patients (often ineptly) are instructive.

One study published in 2008 tracked conversations between hundreds of cancer patients and oncologists. Researchers analyzed how the doctors responded to patients, categorizing their responses as either "continuers" or "terminators" of any given conversation. Doctors were said to continue a conversation when their remarks ran along the lines of, "I can imagine how scary this must be for you," or "Tell me what you understand about your illness." Such a response encouraged patients to keep talking and expressing their concerns. Doctors were said to terminate conversations when they made comments like, "Give us time; we are getting there," which signaled that there was nothing more to talk about. In this study of four hundred doctor-patient interactions, physicians terminated the conversations nearly 80 percent of the time.

The findings had clear medical implications. That is especially so in view of other research indicating that when a doctor expresses empathy, a cancer patient is better able to cope with both the illness and the treatment, which can have positive medical results. (Denise Grady of the *New York Times* described the research, together with a personal account of the exceptional care given to her sister by such an oncologist.) But there are broader applications as well.

Continuers invite honest discussion; they build ideas. Terminators pour cold water on conversations; they kill off ideas. And it's very easy to chase away ideas that might flow from a conversation without being fully aware you're doing so. Think of how many times a higher-up has responded to someone's thoughts by saying, in these or subtler words, "I have a better idea." A more productive response might be, "How could we rub our two ideas together and come up with something new?"

Other notorious terminators of conversation include, "We've been there, done that," or conversely, "We've never done that before," "That's not going to work," or "That's Joe's issue; he owns that one" (which is a particularly unproductive terminator when Joe isn't, in fact, doing anything). Charlie Hawkins, a specialist in small-group communications, has come up with a very useful list of "idea-busters" and "idea-builders." A buster might be "Great idea, but not for us"; its builder counterpart would be "Great idea—how can we make it work for us?" "It's been done to death" would be better scrapped in favor of "Let's do it better or differently." And instead of saying "It doesn't solve the problem," you might want to respond, "Let's connect this back to the problem." And so on.

There are also nonverbal ways of terminating ideas, such as with a facial expression or form of body language that indicates dismissal out of hand. It's better to pay attention to the speaker, show interest in the idea, absorb the thought, and mine the value of it—*before* responding.

More subtle terminators of ideas involve the context of a discussion or the status of the people involved. Leaders in particular have to watch out for the effects of rank on a conversation. It's too easy to unconsciously pull rank, for example, by starting off a conversation with an assertion rather than a question. Stating, "I think the sales plan that we talked about at the meeting is going to be the way to go," is an idea buster. Try asking, "What's your take on the new sales plan?" instead.

Producers of weekly television dramas and comedies understand very well that hierarchy must be neutralized if they want conversations to yield exceptional ideas. The scripts for those shows are usually crafted in what are called "writers rooms," often a hotel room where the writing staff hammers out ideas for episodes. Though the participants are seldom of the same rank—they might include rookie writers, midlevel writers and producers, and co-executive producers—the rule is that everyone has an equal right to contribute ideas.

Deric A. Hughes, a writer for the science fiction series *Warehouse 13*, told of an executive producer who announced emphatically on the first day of work, "Here, inside the writers room, I don't care about a person's rank. I just want to hear good ideas. And if you don't have any good ideas, I'll find someone else that does." Himself one of the mid-level writers, Hughes was quick to explain in a June 2010 interview with Marc Bernardin for the science fiction blog *io9*: "Now, of course, he didn't mean that you shouldn't respect a person's rank and history, but it should never preclude you from coming up with ideas and sharing them with the room. So when he said that, I think this immediately broke the ice and allowed everyone to relax, be themselves, and focus on coming up with great stories to tell."

One of our premises is that all ideas should be welcomed, though not every idea can or should be acted upon. To arrive at a single innovation, you generally need bursts of ideas from all directions. Conversations are a prototypical way of triggering the crossfire of ideas, but an exchange will not bear fruit if people fear that their ideas will be declared dead on arrival, swept aside as wild, or denounced as dumb. Another writer, Javier Grillo-Marxuach of ABC's *Lost* and ABC Family's *The Middleman*, drove home the point:

> One of the things I absolutely believe that no writers room
> should be without is a stupid stick. A stupid stick is a device
> that, when held by the person that's pitching, shields that person from ridicule. I find that it's actually the most useful tool
> I've ever seen in a writers room. A lot of the time, especially
> in the early going, people feel very unsafe, just talking about
> themselves, talking about any number of things. Like they're
> *gonna* be mocked. I generally believe that the writers room has
> to be safe. A good stupid stick allows people to believe that
> they're protected.

For those of us who are not television writers, the stick is optional. The important thing is for the environment to feel safe, so that people will open up and share their ideas. When you're at a meeting, do you feel free to hold forth with the stupid stick in hand, literally or otherwise? In your conversations, are people pouring out ideas as though they were assuredly wielding the stick?

The Value of a Naïve Question

Creating great conversations is not just about avoiding terminators. It's also about finding ways to affirmatively advance a conversation and bring valuable ideas to the surface. Each of us will have a particular way of engaging people in productive conversations. But there are some basics. Listening is indispensable, and giving as well as receiving is a must, because conversations are a two-way street, which means you're both getting ideas and helping others find them. That's simple enough. It's mainly a matter of keeping in mind that the conversation is not all about you and your Hunt. But another critical tool for creating conversations may require extra effort: asking good questions.

Some questions are designed to attract ideas; others are more likely to deter them. Generally speaking, open-ended questions are preferable. "Don't you think they're going to have a hard time hitting their sales target?" for example, is *not* an open-ended question. It is a leading question and quite possibly a terminator. Intentionally or not, the person asking this question is signaling that he wants to hear a particular answer and is not interested in the free-ranging thoughts of his conversation partner. The open-ended version of that question might be, "What are your thoughts about the team and its sales targets?"

Real questions flow out of genuine interest and curiosity. They're not assertions or demands masquerading as questions. And the great questions—the ones that propel innovation—will often come out of left field and surprise people. They might come from a person with a fresh perspective on the matter, perhaps a younger colleague or a new employee.

Innovation consultant Paul Sloane tells of a newly appointed vice president of marketing at a well-known pen manufacturer. At his first monthly executive meeting, he kept hearing the same question: "How can we increase our pen sales?" On the face of it, the question seemed fair and open-ended. At the next meeting, however, the VP told members of the executive board that he thought they were asking the wrong question. He said they should be asking: "What business are we in?"

His suggestion was not well received at first. The executive team felt it knew quite well what business it was in, thank you very much. But the new VP kept pushing. He said he had been asking lots of questions about why customers buy the company's products and came to see that the pens were being purchased less often for their use as writing implements and more often because they could be given as gifts—to a coworker at Christmas time or a student at graduation, for example. The VP had gleaned from his month of open-ended questioning that, "We are not in the pen business but the gift business. We should change our pricing, our promotions, our distribution, and our marketing to recognize this." Sloane reports, in his book *The Leader's Guide to Lateral Thinking Skills,* that once the company accepted this insight, it became much more successful.

Asking how the company could jack up its pen sales was not open-ended enough. The question needed to be the first of many that progressively widened the lens through which the executive team was looking. And apparently the existing team could not do that by itself. It needed a fresh voice, someone who would, in between those monthly meetings, continue to raise simple, wet-behind-the-ears questions like the ones the new VP kept asking. His questions about why customers buy the products were tantamount to asking: *What are we doing here, anyway? What are we selling?*

If these sound like naïve questions, it's because they are—and for that reason, they're important. Never underestimate the value of what might be called a "naïve expert." This is someone who asks the right questions not *despite* his or her lack of formal expertise and experience but *because* of it. Such a person is usually more comfortable asking questions like "Why are we even doing this?" The actual experts may be too immersed in the details or enamored of past success to go back to basics.

We've learned from Bill's friend, the Swiss psychiatrist and balloonist Bertrand Piccard, who piloted the first balloon to fly nonstop around the world. Piccard has more than a passing interest in ideas about such matters as how to increase the buoyant force of a hot-air balloon. They literally keep him aloft. And when he thinks the person he's talking to is naïve or unschooled in some way, he relies on a simple device. When tempted to terminate the conversation, he asks himself: *What if he/she is right?* That almost always does the trick, and he stays engaged, continuing the conversation and raising the probability of getting a new or better idea.

Keep an ear out for the naïve participant in a conversation. The pen company that did so was able not only to boost sales but also to refashion its purpose and brand. It was able to reinvent its gig.

Preparing for the Big Conversation

What shouldn't be missed in the story of the pen company is that much of the action happened offstage—outside of the monthly executive meetings. And there was much to be done. After that first meeting, the VP spent weeks asking questions and getting answers before trying to jumpstart a new conversation with the executive board. He had to prepare himself for the big conversation.

By "big" conversations we mean "very important" conversations, not necessarily long ones. Our friend, Howard Weinberg of Deloitte Consulting, tells of a five-minute conversation he had with a highly influential executive committee member of one of the world's best-known credit card companies. Weinberg wanted to talk to the division president about an idea for an e-commerce joint venture between this credit card company and a Deloitte client in the media industry. An assistant at the credit card company had recommended that Weinberg call the division president early the next morning, while he was driving to work. (The credit card firm was not a Deloitte client at that time.)

"So we got ready," Weinberg said, referring to his Deloitte team. "The day before, we started at about four in the afternoon. We got our team together, and we spent four hours scripting a five-minute conversation." He adds, "We took it as seriously as if we were doing a two-hour PowerPoint presentation."

Keep in mind that Weinberg and Deloitte had arrived at the idea for this venture prior to setting up the five-minute conversation. They had been preparing for an overture to the credit card company for some time. "Just one idea," he stresses—"and getting that idea requires sifting through a lot of ideas, talking to a lot of people, collaborating with a lot of your partners, people outside the firm, shaping ideas until you really feel like you've got something interesting to talk about. And then doing the preparation, the research, getting the specifics, so that you can have a really great conversation. And whichever way the client wants to take the conversation, you're prepared to explore that." Doing their homework paid off for Deloitte. The credit card executive accepted the idea, and the two companies began working on the joint venture.

Conversations are happening offstage, onstage, at all points of an idea process. Why not look ahead to those conversations and collect some thoughts in advance? Big conversations obviously require the biggest preparation. But the little ones may be worth preparing for, too. If you know you'll be seeing a particular individual at an upcoming event, why not think of a good question to ask? Perhaps it will spark a response that adds to your understanding of something.

And despite our earlier caution, what you say doesn't necessarily have to be a question. A statement or an assertion or even a provocation is fine—as long as the parties to the conversation understand that it is meant as a continuer, not as a terminator. That's essential. In an organization, it will depend on the culture of the place—whether, for example, everyone knows that a manager is not tethered to an opinion just because he has expressed it. To launch a steady exchange of ideas, an opinion or a proposal should be offered in what might be called a questioning spirit.

———

Conversations are complex animals. When you speak with someone, you are encountering the thoughts of not just that person but also, indirectly, those of the untold numbers of people with whom your discussion partner has spoken in the past, people whose words and thoughts have become integrated into her own words and thoughts. In turn, you're also speaking indirectly to the people with whom she will have future conversations.

In one exchange, therefore, you could be receiving ideas from many people and influencing the thoughts of many others. Those ideas are themselves products or collections of earlier thoughts and perspectives. They come from somewhere. They're usually combinations of already-existing ideas, and as you set them in conversational motion, they become elements of other people's ideas.

In a sense, all of idea work is a conversation. Idea Hunters converse with people who cross their paths, of course. But they also are in conversation with the magazines they read, the speakers they hear, and the documentaries they see. They are posing questions, drawing connections, and thinking critically about the content. Perhaps most profoundly, they are in an ongoing conversation with themselves. What sorts of ideas am I looking for? What could this particular idea do for me and my projects? How am I progressing in the Hunt?

Perhaps the best advice we can offer to someone embarking on the Hunt consists of just three words: begin the conversation.

Thoreau and the I-D-E-A Assessment

ANDY LIVES IN Concord, Massachusetts, not far from Walden Pond, famed hangout of Henry David Thoreau. You can't pass by the pond without wondering occasionally about Thoreau and his life there. A replica of his little cabin, hardly bigger than a monk's cell, sits just off one of the town's busier local roads. These days, the trail around Walden, which passes by the original cabin site, is a pleasant place for a walk or jog. A public beach, on the shore nearest the road, fills with swimmers and sunbathers in the summer.

Everybody around Concord seems to have an opinion of Thoreau, seeing him as either hero or hypocrite. Acolytes point to his writings, especially *Walden*, and his record as a proto-environmentalist. He studied nature when most Americans were hell-bent on subduing it. Detractors chortle about his frequent walks to town—it's a mere two miles from the pond to Concord Center—and his reliance on family and friends. His mother sometimes did his laundry, and Ralph Waldo Emerson, his lifelong sponsor, owned the land on which he built his cabin. If the critics see him as a proto-anything, it's as a hippie slacker.

If you look beyond the clichés, you learn that Thoreau was neither of those things. He had elements of both: he did love and limn nature, and he had no interest in being hogtied to the respectable trades of the day—doctor, lawyer, teacher, minister. He wanted to write, following his curiosity wherever it took him, though his days in town were split between the family pencil-making business and the gardening and carpentry that he did for Emerson and others. Neither a hero nor hypocrite, he was something else, in our appraisal—a prototypical Idea Hunter.

As he famously put it in *Walden*: "I went to the woods because I wished to live deliberately, to front only the essential facts of life, and see if I could not learn what it had to teach, and not, when I came to die, discover that I had not lived."

Thoreau is one of the most brilliant figures in the history of American literature, a writer and thinker whom many have described as a creative genius—and a solitary one, at that. But a closer look at his life and habits reveal that his ideas didn't come from just sitting alone in his cabin or staring at the foliage. Thoreau had ideas because he went looking for them; he embodied the four I-D-E-A principles in this book.

He was *interested*. He moved to the pond to experiment with living what philosophers call an examined life. On his walks in the woods, he collected specimens to share with the Harvard professor Louis Agassiz, one of the fathers of American paleontology. On his visits to town, he borrowed books and read newspapers and engaged in conversation.

His sources of information were *diverse*. He studied everything from land surveying to ants and ice floes; he invented a new means of making pencil lead. He was insatiably curious, looking for ideas to further his gig—which was to live simply but fully.

He was *exercised*: He wrote seven drafts of *Walden*. He lectured on his ideas, trying them out on audiences before writing them down. His books, essays, articles and poems fill twenty volumes.

He was *agile.* He constantly put himself in the flow of ideas, shifting from lake to town, from books to nature, from contemplation to practical pursuits. And he developed his ideas not in his own brain, or in his cabin, but in close conversation with other members of Concord's extraordinary literary community. These included Emerson, Louisa May Alcott, Nathanial Hawthorne, Margaret Fuller, and others.

Henry David Thoreau is the last of the Idea Hunters you'll meet in this book. You've encountered many others and learned how they've committed themselves to capturing, organizing, sharing, and using (and reusing) ideas.

You've seen inventor Thomas Edison fill 2,500 notebooks with the results of his searching. You've heard how retailer Sam Walton swiped insights from competitors, visiting their stores and quizzing their employees. You've learned how choreographer Twyla Tharp collected her sources and ideas in cardboard boxes, so she'd never forget them and could quickly access them.

Now it's time to test yourself to see how you're progressing in the Hunt. You'll finish the quiz below with a score—a number from 20 to 100. The questions are grouped thematically, according to the I-D-E-A principles. There are twenty. For each, rank yourself on a scale from 1 to 5 and then add up your answers for a final tally. A perfect score—5 x 20—is 100, just like in school. Once you've got your score, we'll say a few words about what it all means.

Interested

	Never (1 pt.)	Rarely (2 pts.)	Sometimes (3 pts.)	Often (4 pts.)	Usually (5 pts.)
I am intensely interested in my chosen field and am always looking for ideas about how to improve my work.					
I try to learn from people, inquiring about their jobs, interests, and experiences.					
I read books and magazines, watch documentaries, and attend talks, just out of curiosity.					
I'm open to my colleagues' ideas, trying to understand them before I criticize them.					
At meetings, I don't just make statements. I ask questions for purposes of learning.					

Interested Total Points (5 – 25) _____

Diverse

	Never (1 pt.)	Rarely (2 pts.)	Sometimes (3 pts.)	Often (4 pts.)	Usually (5 pts.)
I seek new ideas outside of work—in museums, stores, wherever I might be.					
At work, I try to develop ties to people outside of my group or department, because I want to hear different perspectives.					
I look in offbeat places for answers when I have a problem. I don't just stick with the usual suspects.					
I find ideas in fields and specialties other than my own, and I apply them to my projects.					
I seek out projects that might expand my "circle of competence"—my areas of proficiency.					

Diverse Total Points (5 – 25) _____

Exercised

	Never (1 pt.)	Rarely (2 pts.)	Sometimes (3 pts.)	Often (4 pts.)	Usually (5 pts.)
I spend at least 30 minutes a day seeking new ideas.					
I think about my sources of ideas, and which ones are creating the greatest value for me.					
I make a habit of observing and listening; I work at paying attention to people and my surroundings.					
I keep track of what I've seen and heard, finding ways to record my thoughts and observations.					
I put myself in the shoes of my customers or clients; I try to understand their cares and frustrations.					

Exercised Total Points (5 – 25) _____

Agile

	Never (1 pt.)	Rarely (2 pts.)	Sometimes (3 pts.)	Often (4 pts.)	Usually (5 pts.)
I create opportunities to hear my colleagues' ideas, inter-cepting folks at the coffee pot and in the cafeteria.					
I can move fast in response to a need for a creative solution.					
I disseminate ideas—blogging, Tweeting, writing articles or just discussing them with colleagues.					
I "prototype" ideas, putting them in forms that I can test and others can respond to.					
I can eliminate some of my ideas, which enables me to focus on the ones with the greatest promise or priority.					

Agile Total Points (5 – 25) _____

I   _____

D _____

E _____

A _____

Total Points _____ (20–100)

Tally your number. Did you ace a category? Did you tank in another? Few of us excel at all aspects of Idea Hunting. Maybe you're exhibiting deep interest in what colleagues have to say but not casting your net widely enough beyond your own organization or specialized field. Maybe you're dedicating time every day to learning and observing the world around you, but spending less time circulating and developing the ideas.

Your score only matters inasmuch as it helps you understand and improve your Hunting. We all like to know where we stand, but Idea Hunting isn't a test to be passed. It's a lifetime habit to be developed and practiced—every day.

REFERENCES

Preface: Why Hunt?

Bailey, R. "Post-Scarcity Prophet: Economist Paul Romer on Growth, Technological Change, and an Unlimited Human Future." *Reason*, December 2001, http://reason.com/archives/2001/12/01/post-scarcity-prophet.

Romer, P. "Idea Gaps and Object Gaps in Economic Development." *Journal of Monetary Economics*, 1993, *32*: 543–573.

Tully, S. *International Documents on Corporate Responsibility.* Cheltenham, UK: Edward Elgar, 2005: ii.

Introduction: Brilliance Not Required

Barrier, M. *The Animated Man: A Life of Walt Disney.* Berkeley, CA: University of California Press, 2007: 256.

Gelb, M., and S. Miller Caldicott. *Innovate Like Edison: The Success System of America's Greatest Inventor.* New York: Dutton, 2007: 47, 96.

Greene, K., and R. Greene. *Inside the Dream: The Personal Story of Walt Disney.* New York: Roundtable Press Book, 2001: 106.

"Her Toothbrush Talks!" *Time For Kids,* March 7, 2008, *13*(20), http://www.timeforkids.com/TFK/teachers/wr/article/0,27972,1718890,00.html.

Israel, P. *Edison: A Life of Invention.* New York: Wiley, 2000.

Kahney, L. "Straight Dope on IPod's Birth." *Wired*, October 17, 2006, http://www.wired.com/gadgets/mac/commentary/cultofmac/2006/10/71956?currentPage=all.

King, R. "A Brush with Fate: The FireFly Makes Kids Tooth-Conscious." *BusinessWeek,* Spring 2006.

Munger, C. "Wesco Financial's Charlie Munger." *Outstanding Investor Digest*, February 29, 2008.

Peters, T. J. *The Brand You 50: or: Fifty Ways to Transform Yourself from an "Employee" into a Brand That Shouts Distinction, Commitment, and Passion!* New York: Knopf, 1999: 9.

Schechter, B. *My Brain Is Open: The Mathematical Journeys of Paul Erdős.* New York: Simon & Schuster, 1998.

Thomas, B. *Walt Disney: An American Original.* New York: Disney Editions, 1994: 241.

Tingen, P. *Miles Beyond.* New York: Billboard Books, 2002: 24.

Chapter One: Know Your Gig

Barrier, M. *The Animated Man: A Life of Walt Disney.* Berkeley, CA: University of California Press, 2007: 256.

Google, "Our Philosophy: Ten Things We Know to Be True." Accessed September 20, 2010, http://www.google.com/intl/en/corporate/tenthings.html.

Himes, M. "Fostering Vocational Discernment Among Undergraduates." Transcript of talk given to Intersections Project at Boston College, May 17, 2001.

Himes, M. "Intersections: Three Key Questions: What Gives You Joy?" Part 1 of 3. August 3, 2004. Food4thought.tv, 11.15, http://food4thought.tv/fft-bin/f.wk?fft.cont.display+@CCODE=himes.

Himes, M. "Intersections: Three Key Questions: Are You Good at It?" Part 2 of 3. Food4thought.tv, August 2, 2004. 7.37, http://food4thought.tv/fft-bin/f.wk?fft.cont.display+@CCODE=himes.

Himes, M. "Intersections: Three Key Questions: Does Anyone Need You to Do It?" Part 3 of 3. Food4thought.tv, August 3, 2004, 11.13, http://food4thought.tv/fftbin/f.wk?fft.cont.display+@CCODE=himes.

Himes, M. "On Discernment: Three Key Questions." Visitation Monastery of Minneapolis, 2010, http://www.visitationmonasteryminneapolis.org/2010/02/on-discernment-three-key-questions/.

Lowenstein, R. *Buffett: The Making of an American Capitalist.* New York: Random House, 1995: 39–40, 146.

Munger, C., with W. Buffett and P. Kaufman. *Poor Charlie's Almanack: The Wit and Wisdom of Charles T. Munger.* Virginia Beach, VA: Donning, 2005: 61, 65, 192.

Peters, T. J. *The Brand You 50: Fifty Ways to Transform Yourself from an "Employee" into a Brand That Shouts Distinction, Commitment, and Passion!* New York: Knopf, 1999: 17, 32.

Simon, S. *Home and Away: A Memoir of a Fan.* New York: Hyperion, 2000: 13.

Thomas, B. *Walt Disney: An American Original.* New York: Disney Editions, 1994: 241.

"What Is Fat Pitch Investing?" *Conscious Investor Knowledge Base,* July 1, 2008, http://www.consciousinvestor.com/knowledge/questions/64/What+is+a+fat +pitch+in+investing%3F+.

Chapter 2: Be Interested, Not Just Interesting

Chafkin, M. "The Oracle of Silicon Valley." *Inc.,* May 1, 2010, http://www.inc .com/magazine/20100501/the-oracle-of-silicon-valley_pagen_4.html.

"Charlie Munger Speech at USC – May 2007" (part 1 of 5), from a speech given at the University of Southern California Gould School of Law in 2007. YouTube video, 8:46, posted by "tsuseno1," August 9, 2009, http://www .youtube.com/watch?v=L6Cy7UwsRPQ.

"Charlie Munger Speech" (part 2), http://www.youtube.com/watch?v=zRKzJ lydWO8.

"Charlie Munger Speech" (part 3), http://www.youtube.com/watch?v=Ykr poLYY-WY.

"Charlie Munger Speech" (part 4), http://www.youtube.com/watch?v=960quL bAZE0.

"Charlie Munger Speech" (part 5), http://www.youtube.com/watch?v=jVjvpZ ZAdKk.

Ford, H., with S. Crowther. *My Life and Work: An Autobiography of Henry Ford.* Garden City, NY: Garden City Publishing, 1922, 65–68.

Gelb, M., and S. Miller Caldicott. *Innovate Like Edison: The Success System of America's Greatest Inventor.* New York: Dutton, 2007: 25, 37, 148, 150, 165, 186.

Hargadon, A. *How Breakthroughs Happen: The Surprising Truth About How Companies Innovate.* Boston, MA: Harvard Business School, 2003: 26, 49.

Harrison, S. H. *Curiosity in Organizations.* Unpublished dissertation: Arizona State University, 2009.

Hopkins, M. S. "Scott Cook, Intuit." *Inc.,* http://www.inc.com/magazine/ 20040401/25cook.html.

Huntford, R. *Scott and Amundsen: The Last Place on Earth.* London: Abacus, 2002: 72, 98–100.

Israel, P. *Edison: A Life of Invention.* New York: Wiley, 2000.

Kahney, L. "Straight Dope on IPod's Birth." *Wired,* October 17, 2006, http:// www.wired.com/gadgets/mac/commentary/cultofmac/2006/10/71956? currentPage=all.

Lowenstein, R. *Buffett: The Making of an American Capitalist.* New York: Random House, 1995, 39–40.

Millard, A. *Edison and the Business of Innovation.* Baltimore: Johns Hopkins University Press, 1990: 9.

Munger, C. "Wesco Financial's Charlie Munger." *Outstanding Investor Digest,* February 29, 2008.

Peters, T. J. *The Project 50: Fifty Ways to Transform Every "Task" into a Project That Matters!* New York: Knopf, 1999: 30.

Schechter, B. *My Brain Is Open: The Mathematical Journeys of Paul Erdős.* New York: Simon & Schuster, 1998: 17.

Schroeder, A. *The Snowball: Warren Buffett and the Business of Life.* New York: Bantam Books, 2008, 173–174, 224, 445–446, 705.

Schwartz, M. "The Church of Warren Buffett: Faith and Fundamentals in Omaha." *Harper's,* January 2010, http://harpers.org/archive/2010/01/0082783.

Sloane, P. *The Leader's Guide to Skills: Unlocking the Creativity and Innovation in You and Your Team.* London: Kogan Page, 2006: 62.

Szwed, J. *So What: The Life of Miles Davis.* New York: Simon & Schuster, 2002: 256.

Walton, S., with J. Huey. *Sam Walton, Made in America: My Story.* New York: Doubleday, 1992: 63, 81.

Watts, S. *The People's Tycoon: Henry Ford and the American Century.* New York: Vintage Books, 2006: 111.

IdeaWork #1

Auletta, K. *Googled: The End of the World as We Know It.* New York: Penguin Group USA, 2009: 18.

"Charlie Munger Speech at USC – May 2007" (parts 1 through 5), from a speech given at the University of Southern California Gould School of Law in 2007. YouTube video, 8:46, posted by "tsuseno1," August 9, 2009, http://www.youtube.com/watch?v=L6Cy7UwsRPQ.

Ditkoff, M. "It's Innovation Time at the OK Corel." The Heart of Innovation, August 8, 2007, http://www.ideachampions.com/weblogs/archives/2007/08/its_innovation.shtml.

Ditkoff, M. "INNOVATION: It's About Time!" The Heart of Innovation (blog), July 23, 2008, http://www.ideachampions.com/weblogs/archives/2008/07/post_3.shtml.

Hamel, G., with B. Breen. *The Future of Management.* Boston, MA: Harvard Business School Press, 2007: 91.

Hunt, L. "W. L. Gore: MarketBuster." Rita Gunther McGrath, May 4, 2005, http://ritamcgrath.com/blog/comments/market-busting-case-studies-and -applications/.

Munger, C. "Wesco Financial's Charlie Munger." *Outstanding Investor Digest*, February 29, 2008.

Oakley, E., and D. Krug. *Enlightened Leadership: Getting to the Heart of Change*. New York: Fireside, 1991: 169.

Smith, N. "Profile: W. L. Gore." The *Institution of Engineering and Technology*, October 21, 2008, http://kn.theiet.org/magazine/issues/0818/people -profit0818.cfm.

"W. L. Gore's High-Tech Elixir Guitar Strings: Using the Coating Technologies That Make Waterproof Fabric and Comfortable Dental Floss, Gore Delivers a Unique and Long-Lasting Guitar String." *HighBeam Research*, June 1, 2002, http://www.highbeam.com/DocPrint.aspx?DocId=1G1:88585945.

Chapter 3: Diversifying the Hunt

Bechky, B. A., and A. B. Hargadon. "When Organizations of Creatives Become Creative Collectives: A Field Study of Problem Solving at Work." *Organization Science*, 2006, *17*(4): 484–500.

Bryan, G. *Edison: The Man and His Work*. Garden City, NY: Garden City Publishing, 1926: 312–316.

Burt, R. S. "Structural Holes and Good Ideas." *American Journal of Sociology*, 110.2 (2004): 349–399.

Coutu, D. "Creativity Step by Step: A Conversation with Choreographer Twyla Tharp." *Harvard Business Review*, April 2008, http://hbr.org/2008/04/creativity-step-by-step/ar/1.

Gelb, M., and S. Miller Caldicott. *Innovate Like Edison: The Success System of America's Greatest Inventor*. New York: Dutton, 2007.

Granovetter, M. "The Strength of Weak Ties." *American Journal of Sociology*, *78*(6), May 1973: 1360–1380.

Hagenmeier, W., A. Holst, and M. Eden. "Vive La Difference!" *Outlook: The Online Journal of High-Performance Business*, June 2010, http://www .accenture.com/Global/Research_and_Insights/Outlook/Outlook-Journal -2010-Vive-Difference.htm?print=true.

Hargadon, A. *How Breakthroughs Happen: The Surprising Truth About How Companies Innovate*. Boston, MA: Harvard Business School, 2003: 49, 149, 150–151, 162–163.

Harrison, S. H. *Curiosity in Organizations*. Unpublished dissertation: Arizona State University, 2009.

Hughes, Jack; founder, TopCoder. Author interview, April 16, 2010.

Israel, P. *Edison: A Life of Invention.* New York: Wiley, 29.

Kahney, L. "Straight Dope on IPod's Birth." *Wired,* October 17, 2006, http:// www.wired.com/gadgets/mac/commentary/cultofmac/2006/10/71956 ?currentPage=all.

Katz, R. "The Effects of Group Longevity on Project Communication and Performance." *Administrative Science Quarterly,* 27 (1982), 81–104.

Koch, Jim; chairman, The Boston Beer Company. Author interview, July 13, 2010.

Kolhatkar, S. "What If Women Ran Wall Street? Testosterone and Risk." *New York Magazine,* March 21, 2010, http://nymag.com/news/business finance/64950/.

Lakhani, K., D. Garvin, and E. Lonstein. "TopCoder (A): Developing Software Through Crowdsourcing." *Harvard Business Review,* January 15, 2010, http://hbr.org/product/topcoder-a-developing-software-through-crowd sourci/an/610032-PDF-ENG?Ntt=Topcoder.

Sarno, D. "Twitter Creator Jack Dorsey Illuminates the Site's Founding Document," part I. *Los Angeles Times,* February 18, 2009, http://latimesblogs .latimes.com/technology/2009/02/twitter-creator.html.

Sloane, P. *The Leader's Guide to Skills: Unlocking the Creativity and Innovation in You and Your Team.* London: Kogan Page, 2006: 62.

"The Boston Beer Company—About Us." The Boston Beer Company, accessed October 15, 2010, http://www.bostonbeer.com/phoenix.zhtml?c=69432 &p=irol-homeprofile.

Welch, J., with J. A. Byrne. *Jack: Straight from the Gut.* New York: Warner Books, 2001: 190.

Welch, J., with S. Welch. *Winning.* New York: HarperCollins, 2005: 185.

IdeaWork #2

Bartlett, C. A. "McKinsey & Company: Managing Knowledge and Learning." *Harvard Business Review,* 1996: 1–17.

Hargadon, A. *How Breakthroughs Happen: The Surprising Truth About How Companies Innovate.* Boston, MA: Harvard Business School, 2003: 65, 88.

Lowenstein, R. *Buffett: The Making of an American Capitalist.* New York: Random House, 1995: 39–40, 64–65, 81–82.

Nanda, A., and K. Morrell. "McKinsey & Company: An Institution at a Crossroads." *Harvard Business Review,* 2005, 1–27.

Rabe, C. *The Innovation Killer: How What We Know Limits What We Can Imagine—and What Smart Companies Are Doing About It.* New York: American Management Association, 2006: 7.

Schroeder, A. *The Snowball: Warren Buffett and the Business of Life.* New York: Bantam Books, 2008: 173–174.

Chapter 4: Mastering the Habits of the Hunt

Berra, Y., with D. Kaplan. *You Can Observe a Lot by Watching: What I've Learned About Teamwork from the Yankees and Life.* Hoboken, NJ: Wiley, 2008: 21.

Deutschman, A. "The Enlightenment of Richard Branson." *Fast Company,* September 1, 2006, http://www.fastcompany.com/magazine/108/open _customers-branson.html.

Dubos, R. *Louis Pasteur—Free Lance of Science.* Boston, MA: Smith Press, 2007: 309.

Garvin, D. *Learning in Action: A Guide to Putting the Learning Organization to Work.* Boston, MA: Harvard Business School Press, 2000: 66–72, 83–90.

Gelb, M., and S. Miller Caldicott. *Innovate Like Edison: The Success System of America's Greatest Inventor.* New York: Dutton, 2007: 84–89, 93.

Heskett, J. L., and W. E. Sasser. "Achieving Breakthrough Value: Putting the Value Profit Chain to Work." Harvard Business School Case Method Teaching CD: 804–137.

Heskett, J. L., W. E. Sasser, and L. A. Schlesinger. *The Service Profit Chain: How Leading Companies Link Profit and Growth to Loyalty, Satisfaction and Value.* New York: The Free Press, 1997.

Kahney, L. "Straight Dope on IPod's Birth." *Wired,* October 17, 2006, http:// www.wired.com/gadgets/mac/commentary/cultofmac/2006/10/71956 ?currentPage=all.

Kelley, T., and J. Littman. *The Art of Innovation: Lessons in Creativity from IDEO, America's Leading Design Firm.* New York: Currency/Doubleday, 2001: 24, 31.

King, R. "A Brush with Fate: The FireFly Makes Kids Tooth-Conscious." *Businessweek,* Spring 2006.

Koch, Jim; chairman, The Boston Beer Company. Author interview, July 13, 2010.

"Learning to See Through Your Customers' Eyes." *FedFocus,* November 2007, http://www.frbservices.org/fedfocus/archive_downloads/fedfocus _november_2007_12.pdf.

McAuliffe, K. "The Undiscovered World of Thomas Edison." *Atlantic Monthly,* December 1995, http://www.theatlantic.com/past/docs/issues/95dec/ edison/edison.htm.

Munger, C., with W. Buffett and P. Kaufman. *Poor Charlie's Almanack: The Wit and Wisdom of Charles T. Munger.* Virginia Beach, VA: Donning, 2005: 182.

Olsen, P. "The Encouragement Factor." *New York Times,* February 14, 2010, http://www.nytimes.com/2010/02/14/jobs/14boss.html.

Pinker, S. "Mind Over Mass Media." *New York Times,* June 10, 2010, http://www.nytimes.com/2010/06/11/opinion/11Pinker.html.

Riggs, R. *The Sherlock Holmes Handbook: The Methods and Mysteries of the World's Greatest Detective.* Philadelphia, PA: Quirk Books, 2009: 184.

"Symposium on Aristotle's Ethics." November 19, 2008, http://aristotle-symposium.blogspot.com/.

Walton, S., with J. Huey. *Sam Walton, Made in America: My Story.* New York: Doubleday, 1992: 48.

Watts, S. *The People's Tycoon: Henry Ford and the American Century.* New York: Vintage Books, 2006: 45.

IdeaWork #3

Boynton, A., and W. A. Fischer. "Are You an Effective Knowledge Professional? Cashing In on Ideas." *Perspectives for Managers,* International Institute for Management Development, Lausanne, Switzerland, May 2002.

Boynton, A., and W. A. Fischer. "IDEO's Tech Box: The Crystallization of Experience." IMD Case Study, International Institute for Management Development, Lausanne, Switzerland, 2003 (IMD-3-1240; v. 27.01.2004).

Hargadon, A., and R. I. Sutton. "Building an Innovation Factory." *Harvard Business Review,* May–June 2000.

Sargent, Ronald L.; chairman and chief executive officer, Staples. Author interview, June 21, 2010.

Sun, Rickson; chief technologist, IDEO. Author interview, April 7, 2010.

Tharp, T., with M. Reiter. *The Creative Habit: Learn It and Use It for Life.* New York: Simon & Schuster, 2003: 20–31, 70–71, 82.

Chapter 5: Idea Flow Is Critical

Barrier, M. *The Animated Man: A Life of Walt Disney.* Berkeley, CA: University of California Press, 2007: 238.

Bernstein, B., and B. B. Haurs, *Leonard Bernstein: An American Original.* New York: Harper, 2008: 65.

Buchholz, T. G. *New Ideas from Dead CEOs: Lasting Lessons from the Corner Office.* New York: Collins, 2007.

Burt, R. S. "Structural Holes and Good Ideas." *American Journal of Sociology,* 110.2 (2004): 349–399.

Catmull, E. "How Pixar Fosters Collective Creativity." *Harvard Business Review,* September 2008, http://corporatelearning.hbsp.org/corporate/assets/content/Pixararticle.pdf.

Garvin, D. *Putting the Learning Organization to Work.* 1996 HBS Video Series. Harvard Business School Publishing, 1996.

Garvin, D. *Learning in Action: A Guide to Putting the Learning Organization to Work.* Boston, MA: Harvard Business School Press, 2000: 66–72.

Hunt, L. "W. L. Gore: MarketBuster." *Rita Gunther McGrath,* May 4, 2005, http://ritamcgrath.com/blog/comments/market-busting-case-studies-and -applications/.

Judson, O. "So Long, and Thanks." *New York Times,* July 29, 2010, http:// opinionator.blogs.nytimes.com/2010/06/29/so-long-and-thanks/.

Kelley, D. "Ideation and Diversity: A Short Lesson from David Kelley." Stanford d.school Design Thinking Bootcamp video, 1:32. September 29, 2009, http://thinkdesignchange.com/?tag=designthinking&page=2.

Kelley, T., and J. Littman. *The Art of Innovation: Lessons in Creativity from IDEO, America's Leading Design Firm.* New York: Currency/Doubleday, 2001: 230.

Lawrence, G. *Dance with Demons: The Life of Jerome Robbins.* New York: Putnam, 2001: 231–247.

Mary Kay Inc. "Mary Kay Independent Sales Force Surges to More Than 2 Million Members; Company Celebrates Achievements During Annual Seminar," press release, July 14, 2009, http://www.marykay.com/content/ company/pr_pressreleases_salesforcesurges.aspx] salespeople; see also http:// www.msnbc.msn.com/id/21033603/.

Peters, T. J. *The Brand You 50: Fifty Ways to Transform Yourself from an "Employee" into a Brand That Shouts Distinction, Commitment, and Passion!* New York: Knopf, 1999: 7.

Rao, H., R. Sutton, and A. Webb. "Innovation Lessons from Pixar: An Interview with Oscar-Winning Director Brad Bird." *McKinsey Quarterly,* http://denitza.wordpress.com/2008/04/17/innovation-lessons-from-pixar/.

Sutton, R. "If You're the Boss, Start Killing More Good Ideas." *Harvard Business Review,* August 27, 2010, http://blogs.hbr.org/cs/2010/08/if_youre _the_boss_start_killin.html.

Thomke, S., and A. Nimgade. "IDEO Product Development." Harvard Business School Publishing, June 22, 2000.

"W. L. Gore's High-Tech Elixir Guitar Strings." *HighBeam Research,* June 1, 2002, http://www.highbeam.com/DocPrint.aspx?DocId=1G1:88585945.

Zadan, C. *Sondheim & Co.* New York: Harper & Row, 1974: 14.

IdeaWork #4

Jobs, S. "Apple Special Event January 2010." Apple, 1:32:46,http://www.apple .com/apple-events/january-2010.

Rogers, E. M. *Diffusion of Innovations*, 5th ed. New York: The Free Press, 2003.

Stern, J. "Among E-Readers, Competition Heats Up." *New York Times*, June 9, 2010, http://www.nytimes.com/2010/06/10/technology/personaltech/10TAB.html.

"W. L. Gore's High-Tech Elixir Guitar Strings." *HighBeam Research*, June 1, 2002, http://www.highbeam.com/DocPrint.aspx?DocId=1G1:88585945.

Chapter 6: Create Great Conversations

Allen, T. J. *Managing the Flow of Technology: Technology Transfer and the Dissemination of Technological Information Within the R&D Organization.* Cambridge, MA: MIT Press, 1977.

Barrier, M. *The Animated Man: A Life of Walt Disney.* Berkeley, CA: University of California Press, 2007: 142.

Bernardin, M. "Inside the Writers Room: Top SciFi Writers Reveal Tricks of the Trade." *io9*, June 7, 2010, http://io9.com/5555114/inside-the-tv-writers-room-a-place-of-magic-and-mystery-and-making-shit-up-for-money.

Gitler I. *Swing to Bop: An Oral History of the Transition in Jazz in the 1940s.* Oxford: Oxford University Press, 1987: 209.

Grady, D. "For Cancer Patients, Empathy Goes a Long Way." *New York Times*, January 8, 2008.

Hawkins, C. "Idea-Busters vs. Idea-Builders." Make Meetings Matter, 2008, http://www.makemeetingsmatter.com/articles/IdeaBustersVsIdeaBuilders.html.

Piccard, Bertrand. Author interview, 2008.

Sloane, P. *The Leader's Guide to Lateral Thinking Skills: Unlocking the Creativity and Innovation in You and Your Team.* London: Kogan Page, 2006: 42–49.

Weinberg, Howard; Deloitte Consulting. Author interview, May 2009.

Epilogue: Thoreau and the I-D-E-A Assessment

Cheever, S. *American Bloomsbury: Louisa May Alcott, Ralph Waldo Emerson, Margaret Fuller, Nathaniel Hawthorne, and Henry David Thoreau: Their Lives, Their Loves, Their Work.* New York: Simon & Schuster, 2007.

Schreiner, S. A., Jr. *The Concord Quartet: Alcott, Emerson, Hawthorne, Thoreau, and the Friendship That Inspired the American Mind.* Hoboken, New Jersey: Wiley, 2006.

Sullivan, R. *The Thoreau You Don't Know: What the Prophet of Environmentalism Really Meant.* New York: Harper, 2009.

Thoreau, H. D. *Walden.* Boston: Beacon Press, 2004 (originally published 1854).

ACKNOWLEDGMENTS

The journey to this book's completion was a long and exhilarating one. In the spirit of the arguments we make in the book itself, we have hunted for, played with, tested, "borrowed," and rejected (usually with great reluctance) a wealth of ideas—ours and, most often, others'—on our way to arriving at the book you hold in your hands (or on your reader). Despite our enthusiasm for both the process and the product, it would be a gross exaggeration to say this book was written by Andy Boynton and Bill Fischer. Many friends and colleagues contributed throughout this entire project. We first want to recognize our colleague and friend Bill Bole. His commitment to the effort ranged from valuable Idea Hunter to superb project leader, but above all his role as a true "virtuoso" writer was essential in creating a book on which we're all proud to have collaborated.

We are grateful for the work done by an exceptional editorial and production team at Jossey-Bass/Wiley. Our thanks go especially to our knowledgeable editor, Susan Williams, who steered us in all the right directions, as well as to team members Rob Brandt and Nina Kreiden. Warm thanks also go to the person who brought us to Jossey-Bass—our tireless agent, Jeffrey Krames. Because we reside on different continents, those to whom we owe acknowledgments literally span the globe. We gained particularly valuable ideas from Jim Pulcrano of the International Institute for Management Development (IMD) (Lausanne, Switzerland) and Marianne Vandenbosch at McGill (Montreal, Canada), who provided important feedback on early prototypes. They accelerated and enhanced the entire effort by helping us conduct a virtual DeepDive, the idea-spawning method that we fashioned for use by corporate teams (it was acquired in 2006 by Deloitte Consulting). We also wish to thank Ville Karkianen (Sweden), Susan Moniz Harrington (Boston), Tina Richards (San Francisco), and Holly Johnstone (Milwaukee), who gave early-stage support along with important and valuable insights. Our friends Howard Weinberg (Deloitte Consulting, New York) and Michael Raynor (Deloitte Consulting, Toronto) never failed to illustrate and stimulate new perspectives on the Hunt for ideas. Bill's love of ideas was also stimulated at an early age by Helen McShane and Denis Moore at Brooklyn's P.S. 104, for which he'll always be grateful.

Andy extends a heartfelt and special thank-you to the Boston College community. His supportive and talented friends and colleagues in the Carroll School of Management always provide wonderful opportunities to "steal" ideas in the most collegial sense of the word. Bess Rouse, Ericka Steckler, and Reut Livine-Tarandach, outstanding Ph.D. candidates at Boston College, added their excellent research skills and creative imaginations to a couple of the "IdeaWorks" items. Sara Wirsul, an equally outstanding MBA student, shouldered a variety of research and editorial tasks from beginning to end; undergraduates Marissa Bertorelli and Daniel Monan rounded out the impressive team of research assistants. (In addition, wordsmiths Tim Gray and Lilith Fondulas lent their fine editorial hands to a few important passages of the text.) In the dean's office, Barbara Burdick and Ann Loscocco were tremendously helpful in pulling all the threads together to complete this book. Being a business school dean at a university on the move is demanding, so a special thank-you is extended to President Fr. William Leahy and Provost Dr. Cutberto Garza, who gave Andy the encouragement and freedom to pursue this serious project while at the same time trusting in his day-to-day leadership as dean of the Carroll School.

At IMD, the project was generously and enthusiastically supported throughout the community. Of special note for their encouragement are Phil Rosenzweig, Jean-Pierre Lehmann, the late Tom Vollmann, Mike Stanford, Tania Cavassini-Dussey, Kevin Anselmo, and Cedric Vaucher. Without the assistance of Rahel Albrecht none of this, or anything else for that matter, would ever have been realized. Carole Prusansky was a huge fan of the project, and Jim McGivney, David Whitescarver, Les Garner, Christian Dussey, and Joe DiStefano added many useful insights. Mike Cohen of UNC-Chapel Hill's medical school and Charlie Fine of MIT/Sloan both listened many times to the ideas in the book and invariably helped make them better.

Bill wants, in particular, to thank Andy for his boundless energy, ambition, enthusiasm, and genius. He has been a good friend, colleague, ally, and brother for nearly thirty years. This book is a living testament to the power of partnership and inclusion: more minds are always better than fewer!

Andy wants to thank Bill for his wonderful friendship and a very special gift. Andy has been an eyewitness to the King of Idea Hunters for over twenty-five years. Bill soaks up new ideas from every nook and cranny around the world and every encounter with folks from all walks of life, translating this avalanche of learning into his gig with remarkable results. Bill is simply this: the world's best maestro of executive education experiences.

This book is truly an illustration of ideas we uncovered through our wide-ranging research and writing. Scholars such as Paul Romer, Mark Grannovetter, Tom Allen, and Ron Burt are among those who stand out as influencing how we think and write about the role of ideas in the lives of today's most effective knowledge professionals. Interviews with thoughtful and top-notch leaders were critical in creating *The Idea Hunter*. Ron Sargent, CEO of industry leader Staples; Jim Koch, CEO and founder of the leader in craft brew, Boston Beer Company (home of the delicious Sam Adams beer!); Bertrand Piccard, who led the first manned balloon flight around the world; and Jack Hughes, CEO and founder of the game-changing software development firm TopCoder—they and others gave us eye-opening insights that we've done our best to pass on to you, the reader. We thank them all for spending their valuable time with us and for being so open in discussing their Idea Hunting strategies. Many of our insights come from people we never met. Special thanks to the many managers and leaders from great firms of today such as IDEO, Pixar, Berkshire Hathaway, and Deloitte Consulting for building terrific firms that liberate their professionals to be valiant Idea Hunters in pursuit of their exciting goals and missions.

Both Andy and Bill want to recognize the executives we have taught over the years while at IMD and around the globe. These classes were our laboratories. In the classroom experiences we created, we prototyped our many ideas in conversation-intensive environments and found out which ones to keep and which to discard. The classes were also our libraries, where each participant was a book stockpiled with energy and insights that gave birth to much of what we know today.

The following all-star cast deserves our special thanks: Marie Annette, Billy, Amy, Kim, Jane, Owen, Dylan, Ian, and Evan. They are our loved ones from the Fischer and Boynton clans who provided us with the freedom, motive, and energy that catapulted us daily to do the very best we could to create a book of which we all could be proud.

Andy Boynton spends most of his time in Chestnut Hill, Massachusetts, as the dean of the Carroll School of Management at Boston College. Working daily with a terrific group of colleagues to shape a business school for the future, Andy has an opportunity almost every day to try out some of his ideas about leading and energizing talented knowledge professionals and experts. In his spare time, he looks for new and fun projects to work on. He is active with research, writes a book now and then, and collaborates with executives in different industries on projects such as strengthening a firm's leadership ranks, igniting teamwork, creating new strategies, and stimulating innovation in challenging bureaucratic settings. Before coming back to Boston College (he's a proud alum), Andy spent over ten years at the International Institute for Management Development (IMD) in Lausanne, Switzerland—simply the best executive education institute in the world—leading executive education programs and founding their global Executive MBA program. He also was a faculty member of the University of North Carolina at Chapel Hill (where he also earned his MBA and Ph.D.) and taught at the University of Virginia's Darden School. Andy now lives in Concord, Massachusetts, with his wife Jane and son Evan.

Their other three sons—Ian, Dylan, and Owen—are at college or in their early career stages hunting for ideas that will create their future.

Bill Fischer has been hunting for ideas for a long time, in a variety of places. Refusing to believe that the world is flat and that, therefore, one place is as good as the other when it comes to finding ideas, he has tried to put himself into places and positions where there is a higher probability of interesting things happening. As a result, he currently is a professor at IMD in Lausanne, Switzerland, where among other interests he specializes in the art and practice of successful innovation and the effective expression of talent. An engineer by training, American by citizenship, and New Yorker by birth and attitude, he has lived much of his life in Asia and Europe. Bill cofounded the IMD partnership program on Driving Strategic Innovation, in cooperation with the Sloan School of Management at MIT. He was on the faculty of the University of North Carolina at Chapel Hill for twenty years, moved to China in 1980, and was the president and dean of the China Europe International Business School (CEIBS) in Shanghai in 1998–1999. He has received awards for teaching, case writing, and research, and in 2008 he received the Imagination Lab Foundation Award for Innovative Scholarship for his writing and teaching on emerging markets. Bill lives in Lausanne with his wife Marie. Their family includes three children and four grandchildren.

William Bole is a research fellow of the Winston Center for Leadership and Ethics at Boston College and an award-winning journalist whose articles have appeared in the *Washington Post, Los Angeles Times, Commonweal* magazine, and many other outlets.

For more Idea Hunting resources, please visit the authors' websites: www.andrewboynton.com and www.fischerideas.com.

INDEX

This constitutes a continuation of the copyright page: